YOUNG ADULT FINANCIAL PLANNING

PROVEN STRATEGIES TO BUDGET AND INVEST WITH CONFIDENCE, DODGE DEBT, AND NAVIGATE COLLEGE & CAREER DECISIONS TO BUILD A SECURE, INDEPENDENT FUTURE

CLAY KENNINGTON

Formatted with Vellum

CONTENTS

INTRODUCTION

When I graduated college, I thought I had it all figured out. I had a decent job, purchased my first home, and started living the "adult" life. But as months plodded on, I realized adulting is hard.

If you're a young adult struggling to make sense of your finances, you're not alone. In fact, a recent study found that a staggering 70% of young adults feel ill-equipped to manage their money effectively.

That's where "Young Adult Financial Planning" comes in. This book is your roadmap to financial independence, designed specifically for the unique challenges and opportunities facing our generation. I've poured my heart into these pages, drawing on my own experiences and the many experiences I've had with young adults just like you. My goal is simple: to empower you with the knowledge and tools you need to take control of your financial future.

Growing up, I knew that debt freedom was important. I dreamed of a great job where I could afford whatever I wanted. I immersed myself in the world of personal finance, listening to every book and podcast that I could find. Slowly but surely, I learned what works best for me. I may still be searching for the perfect career path, but I don't struggle monthly to feed my family. Today, I'm proud to say I've achieved financial independence. I'm debt-free, I have a 5-month emergency fund, kids' college accounts, and I have invested in my future. But more importantly, I've found a sense of peace and security that I never knew was possible. And I want that for you, too. I want to share what I have learned and help you avoid common mistakes.

Throughout this book, we'll dive into the nitty-gritty of budgeting, debt management, and investing. I'll share my tried-and-true strategies for cutting expenses, boosting your income, and building wealth over time. We'll discuss the importance of setting financial goals, creating an emergency fund, and navigating major life decisions like higher education, establishing a career, and buying a home. Remember, financial freedom isn't about getting rich quick or living a life of luxury. It's about having the security and flexibility to pursue your passions, support your loved ones, and weather life's unexpected storms. It's about taking control of your money instead of letting it control you.

There are only three things that you can do with money. You can spend, save, and give. Spending includes the bills and expenses you have to pay every month to live, but it also includes all the things you want to buy. It is important to save money for the future and for emergencies. Giving money to charity, family, and friends in the form of donations or gifts is proven to add happiness to your life. In each of these three categories, your efforts can produce purpose and meaning. Explaining balance and providing techniques are why I wrote this book.

But this isn't just another dry finance book. I've filled these pages with real-life stories, practical exercises, and actionable advice that you can start implementing today. Whether you're a recent high school graduate just starting out or a young professional looking to get your finances in order, I hope that this book meets you where you are.

So, are you ready to break free from the cycle of debt and financial stress and start building the life you've always dreamed of? If so, then let's dive in. Together, we'll create a personalized roadmap to financial independence, one step at a time.

As you read through these pages, I challenge you to be honest with yourself. Reflect on your current financial habits and identify areas where you can improve. Don't be afraid to ask questions, seek guidance, and lean on the support of others. Building financial literacy is a lifelong journey, but it's one that's well worth taking.

So, let's get started. Together, we'll demystify the world of personal finance and give you the tools you need to build a bright, secure future. Are you ready to take the first step?

CHAPTER 1
FOUNDATIONS OF FINANCIAL INDEPENDENCE

Alex just opened a credit card bill to find a balance he couldn't fathom paying off. Despite working tirelessly at his job, he felt trapped in a cycle where payday offered little relief. His story isn't unique; it's one shared by many young adults who feel overwhelmed by the financial demands of modern life. Yet, what separates those who thrive from those who merely survive is often a grasp of financial literacy. This chapter lays the groundwork for understanding financial independence by delving into the elements that make it attainable, starting with the pivotal concept of financial literacy.

Tyler loves his car. It's big, it's nice, and it's fast. The problem, however, is that Tyler's car has him. To make the monthly payment, Tyler always has to fight his schedule for overtime. He doesn't have a choice to work weekends, as he must get all the hours he can to make the car payment...and eat. He can't get sick or dream about other investments, he just has to work to pay for the car. The note he signed requires this payment for 48 months. The remaining balance is dropping almost as fast as its value. Drowning in car debt, Tyler is realizing that there must be a better way. He finally found a buyer, sold the car and purchased a 9 year older model. Tyler is not proud of the new ride, but is grateful to afford life and look to the future debt free. He will get another nice car when he can pay for it.

Anna is contemplating higher education. She would be the first college graduate in her family. Her grades are good and she enjoys learning. Her major concern, however, is the experience of her elder brother who went to college and dropped out. She really wants to avoid his mistake of racking up $60,000 of student loans that he says that he will be paying on for 3 decades. Anna wants college as a springboard into a nursing career and dreams about doing so without student loans.

1.1 UNDERSTANDING FINANCIAL LITERACY

Financial literacy is the ability to understand money and effectively use various financial skills. This includes personal financial management, budgeting, and investing. It's the cornerstone of financial independence, empowering individuals to make informed decisions that enhance their economic well-being. Creating and sticking to a monthly budget allows you to track your inflows and outflows, ensuring that you live within your means and save for the future. Similarly, understanding concepts like return on investment and net worth can guide you in evaluating assets and liabilities, helping you grow your wealth over time. When you possess financial literacy, you're equipped to navigate life's financial challenges with confidence and foresight.

To manage your finances effectively, it's crucial to be familiar with some common financial terms and concepts. Gross income refers to the total earnings before taxes or deductions. Net income is what you actually take home after those deductions. Interest rates are the cost of borrowing money, expressed as a percentage of the loan amount. Annual Percentage Rate (APR) includes interest and any additional fees, giving you a clearer picture of the cost of a loan or credit. Inflation measures how prices for goods and services rise over time, reducing purchasing power. It's why a dollar today buys less than it did a decade ago. Lastly, compound interest is the interest on savings calculated on both the initial principal and the accumulated interest from previous periods. It's a powerful tool for growing investments over time, as it allows your money to earn you more money.

Financial literacy significantly impacts decision-making. It helps you avoid high-interest debt, by recognizing unfavorable loan terms and understanding the long-term implications of debt accumulation. With improved budgeting skills, you can pay yourself monthly payments and prepare for larger purchases wisely. Make sure that you have enough for necessities while saving for future goals. Moreover, being financially literate makes you aware of scams and predatory financial practices, protecting your hard-earned money. You learn to scrutinize offers that seem too good to be true and to seek advice before making significant financial commitments. The confidence to make sound financial decisions stems from understanding these basic principles and applying them to your everyday life.

For those seeking to enhance their financial literacy, numerous resources are available. Online platforms like Khan Academy and Coursera offer free courses on personal finance, covering everything from budgeting basics to investment strategies. These platforms provide flexible learning opportunities, allowing you to build your financial knowledge at your own pace. Additionally, financial literacy workshops are often available through community centers or educational institutions, offering hands-on learning experiences and the chance to ask questions in a supportive environment. Engaging with these resources can bridge the gap between knowledge and practice, helping you apply what you learn to achieve positive economic outcomes. As you continue to enhance your financial literacy, remember that it's a lifelong process. The more you learn, the more equipped you'll be to handle whatever financial challenges come your way.

1.2 THE POWER OF CONTENTMENT OVER CONSUMERISM

Imagine standing in a store, your hands clutching the latest gadget that everyone seems to be raving about. Your heart skips a beat with excitement, but your mind races with a swirl of questions. Do you need it? Will it bring lasting satisfaction? This moment encapsulates perfectly the dichotomy between contentment and consumerism. Contentment in financial planning is about finding satisfaction in what you have, prioritizing needs over wants, and recognizing the difference. It's a mindset that fosters financial stability by encouraging you to live within your means, ultimately allowing for a more secure and serene life. By focusing on essentials and making thoughtful decisions, you can save significantly and invest in experiences or items that truly enhance your life. For example, choosing to cook at home rather than dining out can lead to substantial savings over time without sacrificing quality or enjoyment.

Consumerism, on the other hand, often paints a different picture. It whispers promises of happiness through material possessions, yet frequently delivers fleeting satisfaction. The constant barrage of advertising relentlessly nudges us to spend more, enticing us with images of a lifestyle that seem unreachable. This pressure can lead to lifestyle inflation, where spending increases as income rises, trapping many in a cycle of debt. The more you earn, the more you spend, and soon, those new purchases become the norm, not the exception. A new car, a bigger house, or the latest phone suddenly seem necessary, even when they're not. This cycle can derail financial goals, making it difficult to save for important milestones like buying a home or retiring comfortably.

Embracing contentment over consumerism requires mindfulness and intentionality. Start by practicing mindfulness in your spending habits. Before making a purchase, pause and ask yourself if it aligns with your values and long-term goals. Consider whether it fulfills a need or merely satisfies a temporary desire. Setting personal financial goals that reflect your values can help guide these decisions. Perhaps you value experiences over objects, leading you to prioritize travel or education over accumulating more stuff. Gratitude exercises can also be powerful tools in cultivating contentment. Taking time each day to reflect on what you have, rather than what you lack, shifts your focus from scarcity to abundance. This mindset reduces unnecessary spending and enhances your overall well-being.

Consider the story of Sarah, a young professional who found financial peace through minimalism. Faced with mounting debt and a cramped apartment filled with things she rarely used, Sarah decided to simplify her life. She sold items she didn't need, prioritized her spending, and focused on what truly mattered to her. By embracing contentment, she was able to pay off her debts and save for a future that aligned with her values. Sarah's journey illustrates how contentment can lead to financial stability and a more fulfilling life. When you focus on what truly matters, you free yourself from the endless cycle of consumerism, allowing space for financial growth and personal fulfillment.

Mindfulness Exercise: The Next Time You're tempted by an Impulse Purchase

- Pause: Examine your motivations. Wait 24 hours before you make large purchases.
- Reflect: Consider how this purchase aligns with your long-term goals.
- Ask: Will this item add lasting value to your life, or is it a fleeting desire?
- Decide: Make a choice that reflects your values and financial priorities.

By practicing mindfulness in spending, setting aligned financial goals, and engaging in gratitude, you can cultivate contentment and build a more secure financial future.

1.3 ALIGNING MONEY WITH LIFE GOALS: LIVE, GIVE, SAVE

Imagine waking up each morning with a clear sense of purpose, knowing that your financial decisions align perfectly with your life goals. This clarity is not just a dream. It is a very achievable reality when you understand the power of aligning your money with your aspirations. Defining your life goals is crucial as they serve as the compass guiding your financial journey. This process begins with introspection. Consider what you truly value in life: Is it the freedom to travel, the satisfaction of helping others, or perhaps the security of owning a home? Reflect on your career aspirations. Do you envision climbing the corporate ladder, starting your own business, or pursuing a creative passion? By identifying these aspirations, you create a foundation upon which to build your financial decisions.

Once your goals are clear, it's time to explore the three main categories of financial objectives: living expenses, giving, and saving. Balancing these areas is key to achieving financial harmony. Start by budgeting for essentials and experiences. This means allocating funds for rent and groceries, utilities and experiences. Next, consider how you can incorporate giving into your financial plan. Whether it's tithing to your local church, donating to a cause you care about or supporting a friend in need can bring immense fulfillment. Finally, establish short-term and long-term savings plans. Short-term savings might include setting aside money for a new laptop, while long-term plans could focus on retirement or buying a house. By addressing each of these categories, you ensure a well-rounded financial plan that supports both your current lifestyle and future goals.

The interplay between personal values and financial choices is profound. When your spending and saving habits reflect your values, you experience a sense of fulfillment that material possessions alone cannot provide. Consider an individual who prioritizes giving. For them, the joy of seeing their contribution make a difference in someone's life outweighs the temporary pleasure of a new gadget. Or take the example of someone who saves diligently for travel. Each dollar set aside brings them closer to experiencing new cultures and creating lifelong memories. These choices reflect a deep alignment between their financial decisions and personal values, resulting in a more meaningful life experience.

To help you align your money with your goals, consider creating a vision board for financial priorities. This visual representation of your aspirations can serve as a constant reminder of what you're working towards. Include images and words that resonate with your goals, whether it's a picture of the Eiffel Tower for your dream trip to Paris or a quote about generosity. Regularly reviewing and adjusting your financial plans is also crucial. Life is unpredictable, and your goals may evolve. By setting aside time to assess your progress and make necessary adjustments, you ensure that your financial strategy remains aligned with your evolving aspirations. Use this framework to guide your financial decisions, and you'll find that money becomes a tool that enables you to live the life you truly desire.

Reflection Exercise: Aligning Financial Decisions with Life Goals

- Identify: List three personal values and three life goals. Reflect on how they relate to each other.
- Evaluate: Assess how your current financial decisions support or hinder these values and goals.
- Plan: Develop a strategy to adjust your spending, saving, and giving to better align with your identified values and goals.

1.4 TOOLS FOR THE MODERN BUDGETER

In today's fast-paced world, where transactions often happen with the swipe of a card or the tap of a phone, maintaining a budget can feel like a Herculean task. Yet, with the advent of digital tools, budgeting has never been more accessible or efficient. Enter apps like EveryDollar, YNAB (You Need A Budget), and PocketGuard, each designed to simplify the process of managing your finances. EveryDollar offers a streamlined approach, allowing you to create a monthly budget in mere minutes. It helps track your spending against set budget categories, providing a clear picture of where your money goes. YNAB, renowned for its proactive approach, encourages you to give every dollar a job, ensuring nothing slips through the cracks. PocketGuard, on the other hand, shines with its ability to show you exactly how much disposable income you have after accounting for bills and necessities. These apps enhance your ability to manage money and empower you to make informed decisions that align with your financial goals.

Comparing traditional budgeting methods, like pen and paper or spreadsheets, to these digital tools reveals clear advantages. One of the most significant benefits of digital budgeting apps is real-time tracking. With these tools, you can instantly see the impact of every purchase on your overall budget, allowing for immediate adjustments. Notifications and alerts keep you informed about upcoming bills or when you're nearing your budget limits, helping you avoid overspending. Many apps seamlessly integrate with your bank accounts, automatically categorizing expenses and reducing the manual labor involved in traditional methods. This integration saves time and increases accuracy, ensuring your budget reflects your actual financial situation. While traditional methods may offer a tactile experience some prefer, the efficiency and precision of digital tools make them an attractive option for those seeking to streamline their financial management.

Consistency is the backbone of effective budgeting. It's not enough to create a budget; you must actively engage with it, reviewing and adjusting as needed. Regular budget reviews, whether weekly or monthly, are crucial to maintaining financial health. These reviews allow you to assess your spending patterns, identify areas for improvement, and make necessary changes to stay on track. Consistency also means being honest with yourself about your financial habits and making adjustments when life throws you a curveball. Perhaps a car repair demands an unexpected expense, or a pay raise provides an opportunity to save more. By committing to regular reviews, you ensure your budget remains a living document that evolves with your circumstances.

Selecting the right budgeting tool is a personal decision, one that should align with your lifestyle and financial goals. When evaluating different tools, consider factors such as ease of use, features, and compatibility with your devices. A tool that's too complex may discourage regular use, while one that's too simplistic may not meet your needs. Look for apps that offer features tailored to your specific financial situation, such as debt management or investment tracking. Seek personal testimonials and reviews from users with similar financial goals to gain insight into each tool's effectiveness. For instance, a colleague of mine, who was struggling to manage multiple income streams, found YNAB's approach invaluable for organizing her finances and planning her expenses. Her success story underscores the importance of finding a tool that resonates with your financial habits and goals, providing a roadmap for effective management.

As you explore these digital tools, remember that the ultimate goal is to find a system that helps you understand and control your finances better. It should empower you to make decisions that align with your values and aspirations, offering clarity and confidence in your financial journey.

1.5 DEVELOPING A FINANCIAL ROADMAP

Imagine setting off on a cross-country road trip with no map and no plan. You might eventually reach your destination, but not without a fair share of wrong turns and wasted time. A financial roadmap functions much like a travel plan, guiding you along your financial path with clear directions and defined stops. It's a strategic outline that helps you navigate from your current financial position to where you want to be in the future. This roadmap breaks down your journey into manageable segments: short-term, medium-term, and long-term goals. Short-term goals might include building an emergency fund or paying off a credit card. Medium-term goals could be saving for a down payment on a house or planning a dream vacation. Long-term goals often focus on retirement savings or substantial investments. By categorizing your financial objectives, you create a structured plan that supports your growth and adaptability.

Creating a financial roadmap begins with a thorough assessment of your current financial situation. Start by listing your income sources, monthly expenses, debts, and assets. This snapshot provides a baseline from which you can set realistic milestones. Once you have a clear view of your finances, outline your goals with specific timelines. If you aim to save $10,000 in two years for a car, calculate how much you need to set aside monthly to reach this target. Setting realistic milestones ensures you remain motivated and can celebrate smaller victories along the way. It's crucial to review and adjust these goals regularly, keeping pace with life's changes. No plan is set in stone; flexibility is key.

Life is unpredictable, and your financial roadmap must be adaptable. Consider events like a career change, a new addition to the family, or an unexpected health expense. Each of these scenarios requires reevaluating your financial priorities and possibly shifting your goals. Periodic review of your roadmap allows for timely adjustments, ensuring that your plan aligns with your current circumstances and aspirations. Techniques for these reviews might include quarterly check-ins or annual evaluations, where you assess your progress and recalibrate as needed. This adaptability keeps your goals relevant and prevents discouragement when life throws a curveball. There will be more on the need for emergency funds later in this book.

To assist in creating and maintaining your financial roadmap, numerous tools and templates are available. Online templates offer structured formats for mapping out your financial goals, complete with sections for income, expenses, and savings targets. These resources provide a tangible way to visualize your financial strategy, making it easier to track progress and make informed decisions. Additionally, financial planning software and apps can automate aspects of your roadmap, offering reminders and insights to help you stay on course. Whether you prefer digital tools or traditional methods, the key is finding a system that complements your lifestyle and keeps you engaged with your financial plan. As you develop your roadmap, remember that it's a living document, one that evolves with you and adapts to your changing needs and dreams.

1.6 EMBRACING YOUR UNIQUE FINANCIAL PATH

In the realm of personal finance, there's no one-size-fits-all solution. Each individual embarks on a personal path shaped by their circumstances and experiences. Celebrating these unique financial paths is vital because they reflect personal narratives and decisions that define us. Take, for instance, my college friend who, unlike many of us, chose to pursue a career that paid less but fulfilled a lifelong dream. While his paycheck may have been smaller, the wealth he gained in satisfaction and purpose was immeasurable. He also gained substantial wealth from consistent, purposeful investing. Stories like his remind us that financial success isn't just about numbers but about aligning our financial choices with personal values and life goals.

Personal background plays a crucial role in shaping financial behavior. Our upbringing and cultural influences often dictate how we perceive and manage money. Growing up, some of us may have observed our parents meticulously budgeting each month, while others witnessed a more relaxed approach to spending. These experiences ingrained certain financial habits and mindsets in us. For example, someone raised in a household that prioritized saving over spending might instinctively prioritize building an emergency fund. Cultural norms also play a part. In some cultures, there's a strong emphasis on collective financial responsibility, where family ties influence financial decisions. Understanding these influences helps us recognize patterns in our financial behavior, empowering us to make adjustments that align with our personal aspirations.

Failing to achieve a financial goal can feel disheartening, yet it's through these failures that we often learn the most. Embracing financial missteps as learning opportunities is a powerful mindset shift. I recall a time when a close colleague invested in a high-risk venture, driven by promises of quick returns. The investment didn't pan out, resulting in significant losses. However, instead of dwelling on the setback, he analyzed what went wrong and used the experience to refine his investment strategy. This lesson in resilience and adaptability underscores the importance of learning from mistakes. Each misstep provides valuable insights that can guide future decisions, preventing repeat errors and fostering growth.

Lifelong learning is the backbone of financial competence. In an ever-evolving landscape, staying informed and adaptable is key. Books, podcasts, and seminars are excellent resources for continuous education. They offer fresh perspectives and strategies that enhance our financial acumen. Networking and community support also play significant roles. Engaging with others who share similar financial goals creates a support system that encourages accountability and growth. These interactions can lead to valuable insights and opportunities, whether it's discovering a new budgeting technique or learning about an investment opportunity. In today's digital age, online communities offer a platform to connect and share experiences, further enriching our learning.

As we conclude this exploration of financial independence, remember that your financial path is yours to design. Embrace your unique experiences, learn from every triumph and setback, and remain open to growth. With each decision, you pave the way toward a future that reflects your values and aspirations. This journey is about more than just accumulating wealth; it's about creating a life of purpose and fulfillment. So, celebrate your individuality, draw wisdom from your past, and forge ahead with confidence. The possibilities are limitless when you're true to yourself and committed to your financial well-being.

CHAPTER 2
MASTERING BUDGETING TECHNIQUES

Imagine it's the end of the month, and you realize you have no idea where all your money went. Last week it seemed like you were fine, but now your bank account is barely above zero. This scenario is all too common, yet there's a method that can transform this chaos into clarity: zero-based budgeting. Imagine a system where every dollar you earn has a purpose, a task to complete before it even hits your account. This budgeting method requires you to assign each dollar a specific role, essentially giving every penny a job description. It's a proactive strategy that starts with a clean slate each month, ensuring you're not living on assumptions based on past habits but on intentional, current choices.

2.1 ZERO BASE BUDGETING

Creating a zero-based budget is a straightforward process, though it requires discipline and commitment. Begin by listing your total monthly income. Next, categorize your expenses. These should include essentials like rent, utilities, groceries, and transportation. Don't forget to allocate funds for savings, debt repayment, and leisure activities. Each category should reflect your priorities and lifestyle. Once you've listed all potential expenses, assign a specific amount to each category until your income and expenses balance out to zero. This means that every dollar is accounted for, whether it's for saving, spending, or investing. You might think this sounds restrictive, but in reality, it offers incredible flexibility by allowing you to adjust allocations as priorities shift, ensuring that you're living within your means while still enjoying life.

The benefits of zero-based budgeting extend beyond simple financial discipline. This method fosters intentional spending, prompting you to consider each purchase carefully. By assigning dollars to specific categories, you're less likely to waste funds on unnecessary items. For instance, imagine you're tempted to buy a new gadget. With a zero-based budget, you'd first check if you've allocated funds for such a purchase. If not, you'd need to either reallocate from another category or decide against the purchase, fostering better spending habits. The psychological benefits are equally compelling. Many individuals report feeling less anxious about money because they clearly understand where it's going. One young professional shared with me how this method transformed her finances, reducing her stress and giving her a sense of control she'd never experienced before.

Implementing zero-based budgeting has never been easier, thanks to various tools and resources available. Budgeting apps like YNAB (You Need A Budget) and Every Dollar are designed specifically for zero-based budgeting. These apps guide you through the process, making it intuitive and manageable. YNAB, for instance, encourages users to plan for every dollar, offering a hands-on experience that's both educational and empowering. Every Dollar provides a straightforward, user-friendly platform that helps you track your spending against your budget in real-time. Both apps offer free trials, allowing you to explore their features before committing. For those who prefer a more tactile approach, printable budget planners are available online. These planners serve as a physical reminder of your financial goals, allowing you to see your progress at a glance.

In a world where financial uncertainty seems to lurk around every corner, zero-based budgeting stands out as a beacon of order and predictability. It demands diligence and honesty, requiring you to confront your spending habits head-on. Yet the rewards—financial clarity, reduced anxiety, and a sense of empowerment—are well worth the effort. By embracing this method, you're not merely managing money; you're actively directing it to support the life you want to lead.

2.2 BUDGETING ON PAPER: A MONTHLY RITUAL AMONG PARTNERS

In today's digital age, where apps and automated systems dominate, there lies a timeless simplicity and power in the act of writing things down. Paper budgeting is not just a throwback to simpler times; it's a method that harnesses the tactile nature of writing to foster a deeper connection with your finances. The act of physically recording each expense and income entry engages more of your senses, which studies have shown can improve memory retention and awareness. When you write things down, you're more likely to remember and consider them, allowing your financial habits to shift from the subconscious to the forefront of your mind. This method strips away the distractions of screens and notifications, inviting you to sit with your thoughts and figures, creating a more mindful approach to managing money.

Setting up a paper budget is straightforward yet requires a bit of dedication. Start by gathering materials—a simple notebook, colored pens or pencils, and perhaps a ruler for neatness. The notebook becomes your financial journal, a sacred space where you can track every penny. Begin by dedicating sections to different categories, such as income, fixed expenses, variable expenses, and savings. Use different colors to differentiate sections, making it visually appealing and easier to navigate. At the start of each month, jot down your expected income and allocate it to various expenses. As days pass, record each transaction faithfully. This method helps track spending and allows you to spot patterns over time, which can be enlightening.

The benefits of paper budgeting extend beyond simple accounting. It is a reflective practice, encouraging introspection and fostering a more profound understanding of your financial behaviors. By engaging in this ritual, you're prompted to think critically about your spending choices. Monthly reflection prompts can guide this process. For example, ask yourself: What unexpected expenses arose this month, and how did I handle them? Did I stay within my budget, or did I need to make adjustments? Over time, these reflections can lead to personal insights that digital tools might overlook. You may discover that your weekly coffee shop habit is more costly than you realized, or that you have unallocated funds each month that could bolster your savings.

To make paper budgeting a sustainable habit, it helps to integrate it into your routine as a cherished ritual. Choose a consistent time each week to review and update your budget; for some, Sunday evening offers a quiet moment to reflect on the past week and plan for the next. Enhance the experience by playing your favorite music or lighting a candle to create a soothing environment. Some find it helpful to use paper chains or stickers as progress markers, especially when working towards a savings goal. These small rituals transform budgeting from a chore into an eagerly anticipated moment of reflection and planning. By embedding these practices into your routine, you not only maintain financial awareness but also cultivate a sense of peace and control over your financial destiny.

The example budget below is from Kim for the month of July. The Appendix at the back of the book contains a blank budget for you to copy.

Monthly Budget Worksheet		Young Adult Financial Planning	
Budget For:	Kim	**Month Of:**	July
Prepared Date:	28-Jun	**Revised Date:**	

Monthly Income:

ABC Employment	$ 3,423
Side Hustle Income:	$ 452
Monthly Total Income:	**$ 3,875**

Monthly Spending:

Giving:		Living:		Saving:	
		Housing	$ 1,123	Savings	$ 200
Tithing	$ 400	Utilities	$ 300	Tuition	$ 807
Generosity	$ 30	Groceries	$ 300		
		Transportation	$ 250		
		Healthcare	$ 100		
		Entertainment	$ 175		
		Miscellaneous	$ 70		
		Restaurant	$ 120		
Subtotal	$ 430	Subtotal	$ 2,438	Subtotal	$ 1,007

Monthly Total Spending: **$ 3,875**

*Must be zero **Zero Based Budget:** 0

If you are single, you alone are responsible for your household budget. For the purpose of budgeting, you may consider an accountability partner. This is a trusted confidant for you to explain monthly your successes, stumblings, and needed areas of improvement. If you are married, it is important to act like it and combine all expenses and income into the household budget. Your spouse is your accountability partner, as you are theirs. We named our budgeting meetings the Executive Family Council and have enjoyed great success in our marriage discussing expected income, communicating spending needs and aligning monthly goals.

2.3 AVOIDING THE FRIVOLOUS SPENDING TRAP

You're walking through a store, and a display catches your eye. It's a shiny new gadget or a trendy piece of clothing, and suddenly, you're reaching for your wallet, not because you need it, but because you want it. This is what we call frivolous spending. It's the act of purchasing items that aren't necessary, often driven by impulse rather than necessity. These unplanned buys can stealthily derail your financial plans, one small purchase at a time. Common examples include buying a fancy coffee every morning, subscribing to multiple streaming services you barely use, or grabbing the latest tech just because it's on sale. While these expenses might seem insignificant individually, they accumulate over time, eating into savings and delaying important financial goals like building an emergency fund or paying off debt.

Understanding what triggers these unnecessary expenses is crucial. Often, emotions play a significant role in spending habits. Stress and boredom can act as powerful motivators, leading people to seek comfort in shopping as a temporary escape or distraction. I remember a friend who would binge-shop online whenever work pressures mounted, thinking that new clothes would somehow alleviate the stress. Spoiler: they didn't. The influence of social media and peer pressure also cannot be understated. Scrolling through endless streams of carefully curated lifestyles and advertisements can create a false sense of need. We see influencers flaunting the latest trends or friends posting about their new purchases, and suddenly, there's a pressure to keep up, even if it means stretching our budget.

To avoid falling into the trap of frivolous spending, it's essential to adopt practical strategies that curb the inclination to overspend. Here are three ways to resist impulse buying: 1. Implement a waiting period for non-essential purchases. If you find something you want, give yourself 24 to 48 hours before making the purchase. This pause allows you to assess whether the item is a genuine need or merely a fleeting desire. 2. Use cash instead of credit cards for daily expenses. Handing over physical money makes the transaction feel more real and can deter impulsive buys. 3. Setting a budget for discretionary spending each month and sticking to it can also provide a framework that limits unnecessary purchases.

Case studies of individuals who have successfully tackled frivolous spending can offer insightful lessons. Take Emily, a young professional who realized she was spending hundreds on takeout each month. By analyzing her spending habits, she identified dining out as her primary weakness. Emily decided to set a strict limit on her takeout budget and committed to cooking at home more often. She also started using a cash envelope system for her entertainment expenses, which helped her visualize the finite nature of her spending money. Over time, these changes improved her financial health and helped her develop healthier eating habits. Similarly, Jake, who had a penchant for collecting the latest gadgets, decided to unsubscribe from promotional emails and social media accounts that fueled his tech cravings. By creating a digital detox environment and focusing on saving for a dream vacation, he redirected his spending habits towards experiences that brought lasting satisfaction.

These stories illustrate that overcoming frivolous spending is not about deprivation but about making conscious choices that align with your financial priorities and values. Budgeting is spending the money on paper on purpose before the month begins. It is permission to spend, granted deliberately planned before the need arises. By recognizing triggers, setting boundaries, and practicing mindful spending, you can regain control over your finances and redirect funds towards meaningful goals.

2.4 EMERGENCY BUDGET MEETINGS: STAYING ON TRACK

Picture this: you're sipping your morning coffee when an unexpected email pops up. It's an unexpected expense—maybe a car repair or a surprise medical bill. These moments can throw your budget into disarray, making emergency budget meetings a vital tool in your financial toolkit. When life throws a curveball, these meetings become a space to reassess, reorganize, and recalibrate your financial plan. Situations like job loss, sudden medical expenses, or even a drastic change in your monthly income can trigger the need for such a meeting. Think of it as a financial fire drill—an opportunity to gather your thoughts, evaluate your resources, and create a plan of action to navigate the storm.

Conducting an emergency budget meeting requires a structured approach to be effective. Start by setting a clear agenda to keep the discussion focused and productive. Outline the key points you need to address, such as current financial standings, immediate expenses, and potential areas for budget adjustments. Where can you reallocate expenses to still add up to zero? Prioritizing expenses becomes crucial during these meetings. Identify non-essential spending that can be reduced or temporarily eliminated, allowing you to allocate funds to more pressing needs. You may have to omit next week's restaurant night because of the unforeseen bill. Consider discussing potential income sources or side gigs that might help bridge any financial gaps. It's also important to review your savings and determine how much you can realistically dip into without jeopardizing future financial goals. By the end of the meeting, you should have a clear action plan to guide your financial decisions moving forward.

Open communication is the backbone of any successful budget meeting, especially in shared financial situations. If married, discussing finances with your spouse requires an environment of transparency and collaboration. Active listening, where each party is fully engaged and receptive to the other's concerns and ideas, is essential. Make it a point to express your thoughts and feelings honestly with empathy and understanding. Collaborative budgeting tools, such as shared spreadsheets or budgeting apps, can facilitate this process. These tools provide a visual representation of your budget, making it easier for everyone involved to understand the current financial landscape and contribute to the discussion. By working together, you can identify solutions that benefit all parties and strengthen your collective financial resilience.

Maintaining financial resilience is not just about responding to emergencies; it's about preventing them. Regular budget reviews play an integral role in this proactive approach. Establishing a routine for checking your financial health allows you to catch potential issues before they escalate. Schedule monthly or quarterly reviews to assess your spending patterns, savings progress, and any changes in income. During these reviews, take the time to evaluate whether your current budget aligns with your financial goals and make adjustments as needed. Building a buffer fund is another crucial aspect of financial resilience. This fund acts as a safety net, providing a cushion for unexpected expenses and reducing the need to tap into savings earmarked for other goals. Aim to save at least three to six months' worth of living expenses in this fund, ensuring that you are prepared for whatever life throws your way. Having this financial safety net offers peace of mind and empowers you to handle financial surprises with confidence and poise.

2.5 EMOTIONAL INTELLIGENCE IN BUDGETING

You might not realize it, but emotions play a huge role in financial decision-making. Emotional intelligence, or EI, is the ability to understand and manage your emotions and the emotions of others. In the context of budgeting, this means recognizing how your feelings influence spending and saving habits. Have you ever bought something because it made you feel good, only to regret it later? That's a classic example of emotions driving financial choices. By enhancing your EI, you can make more rational decisions, leading to better financial outcomes. When you understand your emotional triggers, like stress or excitement, you can anticipate how they might affect your spending. For instance, if stress leads you to splurge on unnecessary items, being aware of this pattern empowers you to find healthier coping mechanisms that don't strain your budget.

Developing emotional intelligence is a skill that can greatly benefit your financial health. One effective strategy is journaling to track emotional triggers related to spending. Start by noting your emotions before and after making purchases. Over time, patterns will emerge, revealing the emotional states that prompt you to spend impulsively. This awareness can help you pause and reflect before making purchases in the future. Mindfulness exercises are another powerful tool for enhancing self-regulation. Practices like meditation or deep breathing can help you maintain composure during stressful moments, reducing the likelihood of making emotion-driven financial decisions. By centering yourself, you create a space to evaluate whether a purchase aligns with your long-term financial goals or is merely a short-term emotional fix.

Incorporating emotional intelligence into your budgeting routine leads to more sustainable financial habits. People who practice emotionally intelligent budgeting often report improved financial outcomes. For example, consider someone who recognizes that their impulse buys are often triggered by feelings of inadequacy. By addressing the root cause of these emotions, they can shift their focus from acquiring more possessions to appreciating what they already have. This curtails unnecessary spending and fosters a deeper sense of contentment with their financial situation. As a result, they can allocate more resources towards savings and investments, ultimately building a more secure financial future. Emotionally intelligent budgeting transforms how you view money, encouraging a more mindful and intentional approach that prioritizes long-term stability over fleeting satisfaction.

To integrate emotional intelligence into your financial planning, consider engaging in exercises and activities that enhance emotional decision-making. Create budgeting scenarios that challenge you to navigate emotional triggers. For instance, imagine you receive an unexpected bonus at work. The immediate temptation might be to splurge on something extravagant, but instead, practice pausing to consider alternative uses for the money. Could it bolster your emergency fund, pay down debt, or be invested for future growth? Another activity could involve role-playing potential financial conversations with a partner or friend. By practicing responses to common financial stressors, you reinforce habits that prioritize rationality over emotion. These exercises prepare you for real-world financial challenges and build the emotional resilience needed to maintain financial discipline.

2.6 CUSTOMIZING YOUR BUDGET FOR IRREGULAR INCOME

For many young adults, especially those who work as freelancers, in the gig economy, or rely on commissions, budgeting can feel like a daunting task. Unlike the predictability of a regular paycheck, irregular income fluctuates month to month, making financial planning challenging. One month, you might find yourself with an abundance of funds, while the next, things might be tight. This lack of consistency can create stress and uncertainty, complicating efforts to save or invest. Consider a freelance graphic designer who might earn a substantial sum from a big project one month, only to face a dry spell the next. This unpredictability means they must budget differently than someone with a steady income.

Creating a flexible budget is crucial for managing irregular income without sacrificing financial stability. The first step is establishing a baseline budget for essential expenses. Identify your fixed costs, like rent, utilities, and groceries—expenses that remain consistent regardless of your income fluctuations. This baseline forms the foundation of your budget, ensuring you cover your necessities first. Once you've covered the essentials, focus on creating a buffer fund to help during lean months. This fund acts as a financial cushion, allowing you to maintain your lifestyle even when your income dips. Aim to save a portion of your income during high-earning months, contributing to this buffer fund regularly. By planning for these fluctuations, you can avoid financial stress and maintain stability even when income varies.

Forecasting and planning play pivotal roles in managing finances with irregular income. Forecasting involves predicting income trends based on historical data, helping you anticipate periods of high and low earnings. Look at your past six to twelve months of income to identify patterns or seasonal fluctuations. For example, if you're a wedding photographer, you might notice higher earnings in the spring and summer months. Use this information to plan your budget accordingly, allocating more funds to savings during peak seasons. Additionally, set realistic financial goals that consider your income variability, adjusting them as your earnings change. This proactive approach keeps you prepared for both prosperous and challenging times.

Fortunately, there are numerous tools and resources available to assist those managing irregular income. Budgeting apps like PocketGuard and Goodbudget offer features tailored for variable earnings. PocketGuard, for instance, provides a clear overview of your finances, helping you track spending and identify areas to cut back during lean months. Goodbudget allows for manual entry, which can be beneficial for those whose income doesn't sync easily with bank accounts. For freelance and gig economy workers, resources like Freelancers Union offer valuable tips and community support. Additionally, software like QuickBooks Self-Employed can simplify tax preparation and expense tracking, providing a comprehensive view of your financial health. These tools, when used effectively, empower you to make informed decisions about your finances, ensuring that irregular income doesn't derail your financial goals.

Mastering the art of budgeting with irregular income is about embracing flexibility and foresight. By understanding your income patterns, setting a solid baseline for essential expenses, and leveraging technology, you can create a financial strategy that adapts to your unique circumstances. This approach allows you to manage your finances effectively and provides the peace of mind that comes from knowing you're prepared for whatever financial challenges come your way. As you continue to refine your budgeting skills, remember that each decision brings you closer to achieving the financial independence you desire. The graphic below illustrates Kim's priority spending plan with her irregular income budget.

Irregular Income Budget
Young Adult Financial Planning

Budget For:	Kim
Prepared Date:	28-Jun

Prioritized Budget Categories				
	1	Groceries	$	300
	2	Utilities	$	260
	3	Rent	$	1,250
	4	Transportation	$	250
	5	Charitable Giving	$	400
	6	Healthcare	$	100
	7	Entertainment	$	175
	8	Miscellaneous	$	70
	9	Restaurant	$	120
	10	Tuition	$	807
	11	Savings	$	200
	12			
	13			
	14	Peaks and Valleys Fund		
Monthly Total Expenses:			**$**	**3,932**

Steps

Prioritize Budget Items by importance

As income arrives, pay down the list item by item

CHAPTER 3
CONQUERING DEBT

Imagine waking up one day to find your phone buzzing with notifications from your bank, not with alerts of withdrawals or overdrafts, but with updates on your growing savings and investments. This is the reality of living debt-free, a lifestyle that transforms your financial experience from one of constant worry to one of empowerment and freedom. Committing to a no-debt life isn't just about eliminating balances; it's about embracing a mindset shift that brings psychological liberation and opens the door to new opportunities. Living without debt means you are unshackled from the anxiety of monthly payments and interest rates, allowing you to redirect that energy into building a future defined by stability and possibility. Studies have shown that those who pay off their debts often experience significant improvements in mental health, including reduced stress and anxiety, and a greater overall quality of life (Source 1). This lifestyle doesn't just change your bank balance—it can transform your outlook and your life.

3.1 DEBT FREE LIVING

To embark on the path to a debt-free life, you'll need to change your perspective and implement practical strategies. Start by visualizing what a life without debt looks like. Create a debt-free vision board filled with images and words that represent your financial goals and dreams. This board serves as a daily reminder of what you're working towards, keeping you motivated through challenges. Next, set strict spending limits and goals. This involves crafting a budget that prioritizes necessities and savings, cutting out excess and unnecessary expenses. Consider separating your wants from your needs and allocate funds accordingly. Hold yourself accountable by regularly reviewing and adjusting your budget to ensure you stay on track. Remember, it's not about deprivation, but about making choices that align with your long-term aspirations. Developing these habits is the foundation of a no-debt lifestyle, creating financial discipline that becomes second nature over time.

The journey to living debt-free isn't without its hurdles. Social pressures and lifestyle inflation can tempt you to veer off course. Friends planning extravagant trips or the allure of the latest gadget can make it seem like you're missing out. The fear of missing out, or FOMO, is a common obstacle. It's important to remind yourself of the bigger picture. Consider the long-term benefits of financial freedom versus the short-term satisfaction of keeping up with peers. Finding a community of like-minded individuals who share your goals can provide support and encouragement. They can remind you why you started and help you resist the pull of impulsive spending. Additionally, practicing gratitude for what you have can shift your focus from what you lack to the abundance in your life, reducing the impact of social pressures.

Real-life stories of those who have succeeded in living debt-free serve as powerful motivators. Take John, a young professional who graduated with substantial student loans. Determined to break free from debt, he adopted a minimalist lifestyle, cut out non-essential spending and focused on paying off his loans aggressively. He found creative ways to reduce costs, like sharing an apartment with roommates and using public transport instead of owning a car. Over a few short months, John's dedication paid off. Not only did he eliminate his debt, but he also had enough savings to start his own business, a lifelong dream he once thought impossible. Similarly, Sarah, a recent college graduate, managed to sidestep the debt cycle entirely by working part-time throughout her studies and living frugally. Her financial discipline allowed her to graduate without debt, giving her the freedom to travel and explore career opportunities without the burden of monthly payments. These stories highlight that living debt-free isn't just a financial goal—it's a lifestyle choice that opens doors to new possibilities and brings lasting peace of mind.

Reflection Exercise: Envisioning Your Debt-Free Life

- Visualize: Close your eyes and imagine a day in your life without debt. What does it look like? How do you feel?
- Create: Gather images and words that represent this vision. Make a vision board to keep you motivated.
- Reflect: Consider the steps you need to take today to bring this vision to life. What small changes can you make now?

3.2 THE DEBT SNOWBALL METHOD: SMALL WINS, BIG GAINS

Imagine tackling a mountain of debt and seeing it shrink before your eyes. The debt snowball method offers just that—a way to systematically pay down debt, starting with the smallest balances first and working your way up. This approach capitalizes on the psychological boost that comes from quick wins. By focusing on paying off the smallest debt first, you get the satisfaction of checking it off your list, which can motivate you to tackle the next one. It's like cleaning a messy room by starting with one corner: each small success gives you the momentum to keep going. This method is particularly effective because it builds confidence and reinforces the belief that eliminating debt is possible.

Begin by listing all your debts, from the smallest to the largest, ignoring the interest rates for now. This order is crucial because the goal is to achieve those quick victories. Once you have your list, focus all your extra money on the smallest debt while making minimum payments on the others. As soon as that debt is paid off, roll the money you were paying on it into the next smallest debt, and so on. This creates a snowball effect—each time you eliminate a debt, the amount you can apply to the next one increases. Many people find this method easier to stick to than others because each paid-off debt boosts their motivation to continue.

The benefits of the snowball method extend beyond just reducing debt. It's about building a track record of success that propels you forward. Take, for example, a young couple who managed to pay off several small credit card debts in just a few months. Each time they paid off a card, they celebrated by visualizing how much closer they were to financial freedom. This kept their spirits high and their eyes on the prize. They found that as their list of debts shrank, so did their anxiety. The psychological lift from seeing tangible progress is a powerful motivator that keeps many people on track when they might otherwise falter.

Implementing the debt snowball method is straightforward, but it requires discipline. Start by creating a simple spreadsheet or chart to track your debts and payments. This visual aid serves as a reminder of your progress and helps you stay organized. As you pay off each debt, mark it off and celebrate the milestone. Whether it's a small personal reward or simply sharing your success with a friend, acknowledging your achievements helps maintain momentum. It's crucial to keep the process dynamic and engaging so that it doesn't become just another task on your to-do list. By actively engaging with your debt repayment plan, you transform it from a chore into a series of achievements.

Staying committed to the debt snowball process can be challenging, especially when unexpected expenses arise. To maintain momentum, consider setting reminders to review your debt repayment progress regularly. These can be as simple as calendar alerts to check your budget or as involved as monthly meetings with an accountability partner. Having someone to share your goals with can provide additional motivation and encouragement. Adjusting your budget to accommodate debt payments is also vital. Revisit your budget frequently to ensure it aligns with your financial goals and make any necessary adjustments to keep your debt snowball rolling. These strategies help keep you focused and committed, even when distractions threaten to derail your progress.

The graphic below is the snowball debt payment plan for Robert and Jill Smith. They were newly married and starting their 30s with purpose in paying off all debt except their mortgage within 6 months. Thankfully, they had great incomes, some savings built up and overtime with side hustle potential to increase their income in the short-term.

Snowball Debt Payoff **Young Adult Financial Planning**

Debt Snowball for: Robert and Jill Smith
Prepared Date: 28-Dec

Debt	Payoff Amount	Monthly Payment	January	February	March	April	May
Credit Card	$ 6,380	$ 253	$3,100	$ 3,533			
Car Note	$ 12,000	$ 479	$ 479	$ 479	$4,100		
Student Loan	$ 26,000	$ 482	$ 482	$ 482	$ 482	$4,660	$4,780
Home Mortgage	$ 200,000	$ 2,482	$2,482	$ 2,482	$2,482	$2,482	$2,482
Total Monthly Payment:		$ 3,696	$6,543	$ 6,976	$7,064	$7,142	$7,262

The Smiths listed their four debts in a credit card, car note, student loan and home mortgage. The smallest remaining balance was the credit card at $6,300. After continuing to pay each monthly payment, the Smiths sacrificed to pay off the credit card in the second month using a little of their savings account and his performance bonus. Without that payment, the next month they focused on the car and were able to pay it off in month 3 with a side hustle that she found and worked extra. With the two former payments eliminated, they could reassign the $732/month they formerly paid onto the student loan. With that and 9 weekends of overtime he dedicated, they could pay off the student loan within another 13 months. Looking back, they were astonished by how quickly their sacrifice paid off to free up over $1200 per month that they could now spend elsewhere. They also realized their potential for overtime and side hustle could be redeployed for other opportunities. Even though the home mortgage still seems large, they commit to intentionally paying it down and avoiding all debt going forward..

3.3 RETHINKING CAR LOANS: THE CASE FOR CASH

You don't have to have car loans. Nearly every vehicle is a depreciating asset, meaning that they go down in value every month. Car purchases represent a substantial value of the entire net worth of many young adults. It is critically important to avoid leveraging such a big component of diminishing returns. You can purchase a car with what cash you have. It may not be cool or sexy but it should get the job done until you afford one better. Think of this as a temporary move for long-term stability. Pay yourself a monthly car payment until you can purchase what you need outright.

Buying a car often feels like a rite of passage into adulthood, but the financial implications can be more complex than many realize. Car loans often come with hidden costs that extend far beyond the sticker price. When you finance a vehicle, you're not just paying for the car itself; you're also paying for the privilege of borrowing money. This privilege comes with interest, which can add a significant amount to the total cost of ownership. Over several years, even a modest interest rate can inflate the price of a car substantially. According to Experian, financing a car means you commit to monthly payments which include interest charges that, over time, can lead to paying much more than the car's original value. The moment you drive off the lot, your new vehicle begins to lose value, often faster than you can pay down the principal of your loan. This depreciation can leave you "upside-down" on your loan, owing more than the car is worth.

Navigating the car buying process without falling into the loan trap requires a strategic approach. One effective strategy is to create a dedicated car savings fund. By setting aside a portion of your income each month, you can slowly build up the cash needed to purchase a car outright. This approach saves you from interest payments and allows you to negotiate better deals as a cash buyer. Sellers often prefer cash transactions and may be more willing to lower the price. Timing your purchase can also lead to substantial savings. Car dealerships often offer significant discounts at the end of the year, as they aim to clear out inventory to make room for new models. By planning your purchase around these sales events, you can further reduce the cost of your new car.

Owning a car debt-free offers several advantages that extend beyond financial savings. First and foremost, it provides increased financial flexibility. Without monthly loan payments, you have more disposable income to allocate towards other financial goals, such as building an emergency fund or investing. This flexibility can lead to greater peace of mind, knowing that your transportation costs are fixed and independent of market fluctuations in interest rates. Furthermore, owning a car outright reduces overall transportation costs. Without a loan, you're free from the obligation of full-coverage insurance required by lenders, allowing you to choose a policy that fits your needs and budget. This autonomy can lead to significant savings over time, further enhancing your financial stability.

Consider the story of Mark, a young professional who decided to forgo traditional car loans in favor of purchasing a used car with cash. Mark diligently saved for two years, setting aside money each month specifically for this purpose. When the time came to buy, he had enough saved to purchase a reliable, gently used vehicle outright. By avoiding a loan, Mark was able to avoid interest payments entirely. His decision saved him money and allowed him to invest the cash he would have spent on monthly payments into a stock portfolio, which grew over time.

Similarly, Emily, another young adult, opted to buy a car directly from a private seller. By paying cash, she bypassed the traditional dealership route and got a great deal on a vehicle that met her needs. Emily's story highlights another advantage of buying with cash: the strengthening of the private market, where trade-in offers are often poor, but private sales can yield better prices.

As a young married couple, we were once advised that "young families have to have car payments to safely transport kids." Thankfully, we wholeheartedly shunned that advice. We were never going to be proud of an inexpensive minivan but paid ourselves the monthly car payment until we could buy the desired SUV with cash.

Another common misstep involves opting for extended warranties. These warranties often disproportionately reflect financing charges rather than the actual likelihood of repairs, as determined by actuarial risk assessments. It's more financially prudent to plan for potential repairs using your budget or emergency funds, rather than investing in these costly warranties.

These examples illustrate that while the path to purchasing a car without a loan requires planning and discipline, the long-term benefits are substantial. The financial independence and peace of mind gained from owning every car outright are invaluable, providing a solid foundation for pursuing other financial goals. It has been said that poor people ask 'how much per month?' whereas rich people ask 'how much total cash?'

3.4 NAVIGATING STUDENT LOANS: PAYOFF STRATEGIES

As you step into the world of higher education, it may be said that student loans become an unavoidable companion. However, we preach that is not the case. Commit to your future to continue the debt-free decision. Break years, scholarships and tuition reimbursement programs can boost your finances to continue to study debt free. Never take out another student loan by following the principles outlined in Chapter 6. If you have any student debt already, this section will help you to pay it off.

Knowing when to prioritize paying off debt is important. If you have current coursework available that you can pay for, table existing student loans until they accrue interest. Major lifestyle issues like expecting a baby may delay debt elimination urgency. But before you purchase a home, be debt free. Before investing in retirement, be debt free. Free up your income potential by sacrificing now to progress where you want to be. When you decide you are ready to pay off existing student loans, go all in.

Facing $100,000 in student loans might seem daunting, but setting a strategic payoff goal can illuminate the path to freedom. Consider the math: if you're aiming to clear a $100,000 debt within 2.5 years on a $40,000 annual payoff plan, you'd need to allocate approximately

$3,333 monthly. Now, imagine supplementing your income with side hustles to bring in a total of $120,000. Allocating over 40% of this income to your loans could expedite your repayment timeline. Embracing a frugal lifestyle, reminiscent of your college days, could further accelerate your progress. This disciplined approach shortens your debt repayment period and sets you on a course towards a life unencumbered by the shadow of debt, potentially saving you from decades of financial burden.

3.5 THE TRUE COST OF CREDIT CARDS

Credit cards can seem like a lifeline when you're just starting out. They offer convenience, rewards, and the ability to purchase items without cash in hand. They may also be the most marketed product in the history of the world. But lurking beneath these benefits are potential pitfalls that can lead to financial troubles. They nearly always carry rates of high interest working against you. When you make purchases on a credit card and don't pay off the balance in full each month, interest accumulates on the unpaid amount. This interest compounds over time, meaning that you end up paying interest on your interest, and your debt can quickly spiral out of control. Many people fall into the trap of making only the minimum payment each month, thinking they're staying on top of their debt. However, this is a common pitfall. Minimum payments are usually just a small percentage of the overall balance, designed to keep you in debt indefinably and maximize the interest you'll pay. Over time, what started as manageable debt can balloon into a significant financial burden.

To use credit cards responsibly and avoid falling into debt, it's crucial to pay off your balance in full each month. Due to the high interest, paying every balance in full is critical before accruing extra. Identify these balances early in your monthly budgeting process. You may decide to keep your credit card as a tool for convenience and rewards rather than a source of debt. Regularly monitor your credit card statements online. This allows you to keep track of your spending, catch any fraudulent charges early, and ensure you're staying within your budget. The companies that sponsor both debit cards and credit cards are responsible for fraudulent purchases. Setting up alerts can help remind you of payment due dates, ensuring you never miss a payment and avoid late fees. These practices help manage your credit card usage and contribute to maintaining a healthy credit score, which may or may not be crucial for future financial endeavors.

While credit cards offer convenience, exploring alternative payment methods can also provide financial stability. Consider using debit cards or cash for daily expenses. Debit cards act like credit cards but draw the funds directly from your checking account. This allows you to spend only what you have, reducing the risk of overspending and accruing debt. Cash can also be a powerful tool for managing spending, as the physical act of handing over money can make you more mindful of your purchases. Digital payment solutions like mobile wallets can also be set up with spending limits, providing a modern way to manage money without relying heavily on credit cards. These alternatives can help you develop a strong sense of financial discipline and ensure you're living within your means.

Cautionary tales of credit card debt serve as important reminders of the risks involved. Take, for example, Rachel, who found herself buried in credit card debt after years of unchecked spending. Initially, she used credit cards to buy things she couldn't afford, reasoning that minimum payments would keep her afloat. However, as interest piled up, she found herself trapped in a cycle of debt that consumed her finances and her peace of mind. Determined to regain control, Rachel devised a strategy to tackle her debt head-on. She cut up all of her credit cards, set a strict budget, and worked diligently to pay more than the minimum each month. Over time, she paid down her balances. This experience taught her the value of living within her means and the importance of financial vigilance.

If you find yourself in a similar situation with Rachel, consider making a drastic course correction. Cut up your cards and pay them off with urgency. Use the debt snowball from the start of this chapter.

3.6 BUILDING RESILIENCE AGAINST FUTURE DEBT

In a world where unexpected expenses lurk around every corner, financial resilience becomes your armor against accumulating future debt. A sudden car repair, an unforeseen medical bill, or even a short period of unemployment can easily throw your finances into disarray. Without a plan to absorb these shocks, the temptation to reach for a credit card or take out a loan becomes all too real. Building resilience is not just about having money set aside; it's about creating a buffer that allows you to handle life's surprises with grace and stability. This is where emergency savings come into play, acting as a safety net that catches you before you fall into the clutches of debt. By setting aside funds specifically for emergencies, you create a financial cushion that empowers you to face unexpected challenges head-on, without derailing your long-term financial goals.

Enhancing financial resilience requires practical steps that fortify your defenses against debt. One of the most effective strategies is to establish a robust emergency fund (see Chapter 4). Aim to save three to six months' worth of living expenses, ensuring that you have enough to cover essentials like rent, utilities, and groceries in case of an emergency. This fund should be easily accessible but separate from your regular checking account to minimize the temptation to dip into it for non-emergencies. Another strategy to bolster resilience is diversifying your income streams. Relying on a single source of income can leave you vulnerable, so consider exploring side gigs or freelance opportunities that align with your skills and interests. This provides additional financial security and opens up new avenues for personal and professional growth. By creating multiple streams of income, you increase your financial stability and reduce the risk of falling into debt when unexpected expenses arise.

Financial education plays a crucial role in maintaining and building resilience. The financial landscape is constantly evolving, and staying informed enables you to make smarter decisions. Engaging with financial workshops and seminars can broaden your understanding of personal finance concepts, from investment strategies to budgeting techniques. These interactive sessions often provide real-world insights that aren't covered in traditional education. Additionally, make it a habit to continuously update your personal finance knowledge. Whether it's reading financial blogs, listening to podcasts, or attending webinars, the more you learn, the better equipped you'll be to navigate complexities and stay ahead of potential pitfalls. When you approach financial education with curiosity and commitment, you lay a strong foundation for resilience, empowering yourself to adapt and thrive in any economic climate.

To reinforce resilience-building behaviors, consider incorporating exercises into your financial routine. Monthly financial health check-ups can be an effective way to assess your current financial situation and make necessary adjustments. During these check-ups, evaluate your income, expenses, and savings, and identify any areas that require attention. This practice keeps you accountable and ensures that you're consistently working towards your financial goals. Another exercise is scenario planning for potential financial crises. This involves envisioning various financial disruptions, such as a sudden job loss or a major health expense, and developing strategies to address them. By preparing for these scenarios in advance, you build confidence in your ability to handle them should they occur. This proactive approach strengthens your financial resilience and provides peace of mind, knowing that you're ready to face whatever challenges may come your way.

As you strengthen your financial resilience, you're not just safeguarding your present—you're investing in a future where debt doesn't dictate your choices. This foundation of resilience ensures that you're ready for the unexpected, equipped with the tools and knowledge to maintain financial stability in any circumstance. Building resilience against debt isn't a one-time effort; it's a continuous process of learning, adapting, and growing. This commitment to financial resilience empowers you to pursue your dreams with confidence, knowing that you're prepared for whatever life throws your way.

CHAPTER 4

BUILDING A SECURE FINANCIAL FUTURE

Picture this: you're enjoying a peaceful weekend, watching your favorite show, when your phone buzzes with a notification. It's the mechanic with an estimate for your car repairs, and it's far more than you expected. Suddenly, that weekend bliss turns into Monday morning stress. But what if you had a cushion, a financial safety net that absorbed life's unexpected blows without derailing your budget? This is the power of an emergency fund, a vital component of financial stability that shields you from the unpredictabilities of life, be it medical emergencies, sudden job losses, or any other unforeseen expense. Having such a fund brings financial protection and peace of mind, allowing you to face challenges with confidence rather than panic.

4.1 EMERGENCY FUND

Building an emergency fund might seem daunting at first, but with the right strategies, it becomes an achievable goal. Start by setting a realistic savings target. Financial experts suggest aiming for three to six months' worth of living expenses, tailored to your personal circumstances and past experiences with unexpected costs. This target provides a clear objective and helps you track progress. Automating your savings is a powerful tool to build consistency. By setting up automatic transfers from your checking account to a dedicated savings account, you make saving a priority, ensuring that you consistently put money aside without having to consciously act about it each month. This strategy simplifies the saving process and helps you avoid the temptation to spend that money impulsively on non-essentials.

Emergency Fund Calculator
Young Adult Financial Planning

Budget For:		
Prepared Date:		
Living Expenses	Rent Payment	$ 1,123
	Utilities	$ 300
	Groceries	$ 300
	Transportation	$ 250
	Healthcare	$ 100
	Miscellaneous	$ 70
	Entertainment	
Monthly Total Spending:		**$ 2,143**
3 Month Emergency Fund		$ 6,429
6 Month Emergency Fund		$ 12,858
Target Emergency Fund		**$ 10,000**

Once your fund is established, maintaining its integrity is crucial. It's important to distinguish between wants and needs when considering tapping into this reserve. The fund is designed for true emergencies—a necessary car repair, an unexpected medical bill, or covering living expenses during a period of unemployment. It's not for spur-of-the-moment vacations or a new gadget that just hit the shelves. Replenishing your fund after use should be a priority, ensuring it's ready for the next unexpected event. Treat replenishment as part of your regular financial routine, similar to paying a bill or contributing to a retirement account. This discipline helps maintain the fund's purpose and ensures that you're always prepared for whatever life throws your way.

Consider the story of Lisa, a graphic designer who faced an unexpected layoff during an economic downturn. Thanks to her meticulous savings habits and a well-maintained emergency fund, she was able to cover her rent and essential expenses without dipping into credit cards or loans. This financial cushion allowed her the breathing room to search for a new job without the added stress of immediate financial pressure. Similarly, Mark, a recent graduate, found himself with a hefty medical bill after an unforeseen accident. His emergency fund, built slowly over time through automated savings, provided the necessary support to handle the expense, highlighting the importance of having a solid financial buffer. These stories illustrate how an emergency fund is not just about financial security; it's about creating a foundation of resilience that empowers you to navigate life's uncertainties with assurance and grace.

Reflection Section: Assessing Your Emergency Fund Readiness

- Evaluate: Consider your current financial situation. Do you have an emergency fund, and if so, how does it compare to your monthly expenses?
- Plan: Set a specific target for your emergency fund based on your needs. Consider factors like job stability and health needs.
- Automate: If you haven't already, set up automatic transfers to your savings account to ensure consistent contributions.
- Review: Regularly review your fund's status and adjust your savings plan as necessary to maintain its integrity.

4.2 401(K) FROM YOUR WORK

As you step into the workforce, envision your future self enjoying the fruits of your labor in a comfortable retirement. This vision becomes tangible with a powerful tool at your disposal: the 401(k) plan. Essentially, a 401(k) is a retirement account offered by your employer that allows you to save and invest a portion of your paycheck either before or after taxes are taken out. These funds are placed in a retirement umbrella which can focus on long-term growth. Within a 401(k), you may have the option to choose between traditional contributions, which defer taxes until retirement, and Roth contributions, where you pay taxes upfront but enjoy tax-free withdrawals later. One of the most appealing aspects of a 401(k) is employer matching, where your employer matches a portion of your contributions in a pre-tax traditional account, essentially giving you free money toward your retirement. This match is often contingent upon you contributing a certain percentage of your salary, so it's wise to contribute enough to take full advantage of this benefit.

Starting your 401(k) contributions early is crucial for maximizing the benefits of compound interest and long-term growth. Liberally contribute after you have paid off any debts. Compound interest is the process where the money you earn on your investments is reinvested, meaning your contributions and interest are earning more money over time. The earlier you start, the more time your money has to grow. Imagine contributing to your 401(k) from your first job after college. Over the decades, those initial contributions grow significantly, even if you stop contributing later. Compare this to someone who starts in their 40s; they must contribute much more to catch up. This demonstrates the power of time in growing your retirement savings, where small, consistent contributions lead to substantial growth over the years. See the investment graphic in the ROTH IRA subsection next.

Maximizing retirement savings involves strategic actions. As you receive salary raises or bonuses, consider increasing your 401(k) contributions. Even a small percentage increase can have a significant impact over time. Diversifying your investments within your 401(k) is another key strategy. Most 401(k) plans offer various investment options, such as stocks, bonds, and mutual funds. Diversification spreads your money across different assets, reducing the risk of loss by balancing potential gains and losses. Regularly reviewing your portfolio quarterly ensures your investments align with your financial goals. You may adjust allocations based on changes in market conditions or your personal risk tolerance at any time with the investing company's website.

Retirement planning often brings misconceptions and fears. Many believe they need large sums of money to start investing, but this isn't true. Starting small is better than not starting at all, the earlier the better considering compound interest. Consistent, incremental investments, even with modest amounts, accumulate over time and benefit from compound growth. Additionally, fears of market volatility can deter individuals from investing. While markets fluctuate, history shows they tend to recover fairly quickly. It's important to stay committed to your contributions, regardless of market ups and downs. By focusing on consistent investments and maintaining a long-term perspective, you can weather market uncertainties and emerge with a robust retirement fund.

4.3 THE BASICS OF ROTH IRA

Once you've paid off your debts and established a solid emergency fund, it's time to consider a Roth IRA as your next financial step. An IRA acts like a 401(k) but in the open market independent of employment. A Roth IRA is a retirement savings account that offers distinct advantages, particularly in terms of tax benefits. Contributions to a Roth IRA are made with post-tax dollars, meaning you've already paid taxes on the money you put in. The real magic happens as your investment grows over time, each of the contributions and their gains are tax-free. When you reach retirement age, you can withdraw your earnings without any tax penalties, allowing you to maximize your retirement income.

An illustrative calculation is $100 contribution every month from age 25 to 40. Assuming a 10% annual growth rate, the value of the investments at age 65 would be approximately $452,808. If you started another fund at age 45 with the same $100 monthly contribution and 10% annual growth, at 65 the second fund would be approximately $133,789.03. To match the first fund at age 65, the second would have to contribute $338 per month within the 25-year window. This is most illustrative if considered the same growth rate and $100 monthly contribution from age 25 to 40 would be $3,046,270 at age 85 without additional investment.

Investment Growth Over Time — **Young Adult Financial Planning**

Account Projection: James' ROTH IRA

Estimated Annual Growth Rate: 10%

Account Scenario	Monthly Contribution	Start Age	End Age	Growth Until Age	Projected Value
1	$100	25	40	65	$ 452,808
2	$100	45	65	65	$ 133,789
3	$338	45	65	65	$ 452,808
4	$100	25	40	85	$3,046,270

Finding a reputable investment advisor is crucial when setting up your Roth IRA. This individual will guide you through the process, ensuring your investments align with your financial goals. Take the time to interview several advisors to find someone who resonates with your needs and can explain complex concepts in a way that makes sense to you. Your advisor should focus on the net growth of your accounts, prioritizing long-term gains over short-term fluctuations. They should be transparent on their fee structure and how this affects your balances. This relationship is not just about managing money; it's about building trust and receiving guidance that empowers you to make informed decisions about your financial future. Their job is to educate you on how you could manage your money.

Aiming to contribute 15% of your annual salary to your retirement savings is a solid goal to strive for. To calculate this, take your annual salary and multiply it by 0.15. This figure represents the total amount you should aim to save across all retirement accounts, including both your 401(k) and Roth IRA. By diversifying your contributions, you leverage the unique advantages of each account to optimize the offerings of each retirement account. Consistent contributions, no matter how small, accumulate over time, significantly enhancing your financial security. This proactive approach to saving ensures you're well-prepared for the future, allowing you to enjoy retirement without financial stress.

One of the most flexible features of a Roth IRA is the ability to withdraw your contributions at any time, for any reason, without penalties. This provides an additional safety net, but it's important to understand the primary goal of a Roth IRA is to grow your investments over the long term. Ideally, you would let your contributions and their earnings remain untouched until retirement. This strategy maximizes the tax-free growth potential, ensuring you have a robust nest egg when you need it most. While the option to withdraw contributions adds a layer of security, maintaining the integrity of your account for retirement is the wisest course of action.

4.4 UNDERSTANDING RISK IN INVESTMENTS

Investment risk can seem like an intimidating concept, but breaking it down makes it manageable and, more importantly, actionable. At its core, investment risk refers to the possibility that the actual returns on an investment will differ from the expected returns. This can include losing some or all of your initial investment. Market risk, for instance, is the risk of investments losing value due to economic developments or other events that affect the entire market. Inflation risk is another concern, representing the danger that rising prices will erode your purchasing power, meaning your investment returns might not keep pace with inflation. Interest rate risk involves changes in interest rates that affect the value of fixed-income securities like bonds. When interest rates rise, bond prices typically fall, and vice versa. Understanding these risks helps in making informed investment decisions.

Balancing risk with potential returns is a fundamental principle of investing. Generally, investments with higher potential returns come with higher risk. Stocks, for example, have historically offered higher returns than bonds but also come with greater volatility. Looking at historical data, equities have outperformed bonds over the long term, which is why they are considered higher risk. Bonds, with their fixed returns, are seen as lower risk. The relationship between risk and return is like a seesaw; finding the right balance depends on your individual financial situation, goals, and comfort level with uncertainty. Diversifying your portfolio, which involves spreading investments across various asset classes, can help manage risk while aiming for returns that align with your financial goals.

Managing investment risk effectively involves several strategies. One key technique is asset allocation, which divides your investment portfolio among different asset categories, such as stocks, bonds, and real estate. This strategy helps mitigate risk by ensuring that no single asset class dominates your portfolio. Diversification further reduces risk by investing in various sectors or geographic regions. Regularly reviewing and adjusting your portfolio is crucial to maintaining this balance. Market conditions and personal financial situations change, and so should your investment strategy. Periodic reviews allow you to rebalance your portfolio, ensuring it continues to align with your risk tolerance and financial objectives.

Understanding your personal risk tolerance is essential in shaping your investment strategy. It involves assessing how much risk you're comfortable taking and how it aligns with your financial goals. Risk tolerance questionnaires, available through financial institutions or online, can help gauge your comfort with risk by asking questions about your investment experience, goals, and reactions to market fluctuations. These insights are valuable in crafting a portfolio that reflects your unique financial situation. For instance, if you discover through the questionnaire that you have a low-risk tolerance, you might opt for a more conservative investment approach, focusing on bonds and dividend-paying stocks. Conversely, a higher risk tolerance might lead you to invest more heavily in equities or emerging markets. Risk tolerance is also affected by education. The more you understand, the more you can hone in on what works for you. Study alternate investing strategies, but only act on those you find comfortable.

Personal experiences with risk management can offer valuable lessons. I recall a friend who invested heavily in tech stocks during a market boom, driven by the allure of high returns. Initially, his portfolio soared, but when the market corrected, the losses were significant. This experience taught him the importance of diversification and the perils of putting all eggs in one basket. Similarly, North Dakota locals gloried in WLL returns for nearly two decades but lost much if they retained any through Whiting's bankruptcy. Reallocating assets across different industries, companies and methods, one can mitigate the impact of future downturns. These anecdotes highlight the importance of understanding and managing risk, not just in theory but in practice. Recognizing the inherent risks in investments and strategically managing them allows you to pursue financial growth confidently, knowing that you've taken steps to protect your assets.

4.5 INVESTING WITH CONFIDENCE: TOOLS AND RESOURCES

In today's digital landscape, investing has become more accessible than ever for beginners. With a slew of user-friendly apps and platforms, starting your investment journey is just a few taps away. Take Robinhood, for instance. It's an app that has transformed how people approach investing by offering commission-free trades on stocks, ETFs, and options. Its intuitive design makes it easy for newcomers to navigate the stock market without feeling overwhelmed. Similarly, Acorns takes a novel approach by rounding up your everyday purchases to the nearest dollar and investing the spare change. This method allows you to build an investment portfolio gradually, turning small, seemingly insignificant sums into investments over time. These platforms democratize investing, allowing you to participate in the market regardless of your initial investment capital.

Beyond apps, educational resources play a crucial role in shaping informed investors. Investopedia, for instance, offers a wealth of information on various investment topics, from basic definitions to advanced strategies. It's a valuable tool for anyone looking to deepen their understanding of the financial world. The importance of continuous learning through books and podcasts cannot be overstated either. Works like "The Intelligent Investor" by Benjamin Graham provide timeless wisdom on value investing, while podcasts such as "The Motley Fool" offer insights and analysis on current market trends. These resources equip you with the knowledge needed to analyze market trends and assess company performance, empowering you to make informed investment decisions rather than relying on gut feelings or hearsay. Financial podcasts and videos are abundant.

Creating a personalized investment plan is a critical step toward achieving your financial goals. Start by setting clear investment goals, whether it's saving for retirement, buying a home, or funding a passion project. Each goal requires a different approach and timeline, so it's important to tailor your strategy accordingly. Evaluate your risk tolerance and financial situation honestly. Are you comfortable with high-risk investments for the potential of high returns, or do you prefer a safer, more conservative approach? Does your investing timeline allow for market volatility? Understanding your comfort level with risk helps in selecting appropriate investment vehicles and setting realistic expectations for returns. With these elements in place, you can craft a plan that aligns with both your current financial situation and your future aspirations.

Insights from seasoned investors can offer valuable guidance as you develop your investment strategy. Many financial advisors recommend diversifying your portfolio to reduce risk and increase potential returns. This means spreading your investments across various asset classes to avoid overexposure to any single investment. Diversification helps cushion your portfolio against market volatility, as different assets often react differently to economic changes. Listening to success stories from novice investors can also be inspiring. Consider the tale of Sarah, a young professional who started investing with just a few hundred dollars. Through diligent research and consistent contributions, she grew her portfolio significantly, eventually funding her master's degree with the returns. Her story underscores the power of patience, persistence, and informed decision-making in achieving investment success.

Interactive Element: Crafting Your Investment Strategy

- Reflect: Identify your top three financial goals. Are they short-term, like saving for a vacation, or long-term, like retirement?
- Assess: Determine your risk tolerance. How much fluctuation in your investment value are you comfortable with? Use online risk assessment tools for a clearer picture.
- Plan: Outline a strategy that includes your goals, risk tolerance, and the types of investments you're interested in. Consider setting up automatic contributions to your investment accounts to ensure consistency.

As you explore these tools and resources, remember that investing is not a race but a steady progression toward financial growth. With the right knowledge and strategy, you can invest confidently, building a secure financial future that aligns with your dreams and goals.

4.6 THE IMPORTANCE OF DIVERSIFICATION

Imagine standing in the middle of a bustling market, with vendors calling out to you from every direction. Each stall offers something different—fruits, spices, textiles. You fill your basket with a bit of everything, ensuring that if one item isn't to your taste, others will make up for it. This is the essence of diversification in investing. By spreading your investments across various asset classes, you reduce the risk that comes from putting all your eggs in one basket. If one investment underperforms, others can cushion the impact, stabilizing your overall portfolio. Traditionally diversified portfolios often include a mix of stocks, bonds, and mutual funds. Stocks might offer higher returns but come with volatility, whereas bonds provide stability. Mutual funds, which pool money from many investors to purchase a diversified portfolio of stocks and bonds, offer a balance of risk and return, making them a popular choice for those looking to diversify without managing each investment individually.

Mutual funds constitute the vast majority of our personal investment portfolio. We find our desired diversification within a combination of growth funds, growth and income funds, aggressive growth funds and international funds. Our timelines for retirement are currently still several decades out. We continue to contribute regardless of market reactions.

There are several strategies for achieving effective diversification. Dollar-cost averaging involves regularly investing a fixed amount of money, regardless of market conditions. This method reduces the impact of market volatility by buying more shares when prices are low and fewer when they're high. Over time, this strategy can lower the average cost per share and mitigate the risk of investing a large sum at an inopportune moment. Sector and geographical diversification are also valuable tactics. By investing in different industries and regions, you shield your portfolio from localized economic downturns. For example, if the tech sector experiences a slump, investments in healthcare or consumer goods may remain stable, balancing out potential losses. Similarly, allocating funds across various countries reduces exposure to the risks associated with any single economy.

Real-life examples highlight the power of diversification. Consider the story of Emily, who began investing with a focus solely on tech single stocks. Initially, her portfolio flourished, but when the tech bubble burst, her investments suffered. Learning from this, she diversified her holdings to include mutual funds, some of tech companies and others of general mutual funds, cushioning her portfolio against future downturns. Her diversified approach allowed her investments to continue growing and increase resiliency. Another example involves Mark, who chose to invest in both stocks and real estate. When the stock market faced volatility, his real estate investments provided steady income, demonstrating the resilience that diversification brings. These stories underscore how spreading investments across various asset classes can protect against significant losses and promote steady growth.

This approach to diversification, much like filling a basket with various goods at the market, creates a safety net for your investments. By carefully selecting a mix of assets, you prepare for different economic scenarios, ensuring that no single event can derail your financial goals. Diversification isn't about eliminating risk entirely; it's about managing it in a way that aligns with your financial objectives and risk tolerance. As you continue to build your investment portfolio, keep in mind that diversity is your ally, offering balance and strength in an ever-changing financial landscape. With a diversified portfolio, you not only safeguard your investments but also position yourself for consistent growth and financial security. The most important factor continues to be your understanding of what you are investing in.

MAKE A DIFFERENCE WITH YOUR REVIEW

HELP SOMEONE START THEIR FINANCIAL JOURNEY

"The best investment you can make is in yourself." – Warren Buffett

Making smart money choices doesn't happen overnight. It takes guidance, encouragement, and sometimes just the right book at the right time. That's what this book is meant to be—a stepping stone for young adults who want to take control of their financial future.

But here's the thing: Many young people don't even know where to start. They're overwhelmed by student loans, confused by budgeting, and unsure how to build a strong financial foundation. The best way to help them? Make sure they find resources like this book.

And you can do that right now—by leaving a quick review.

Most people judge a book by its cover (and its reviews). So on behalf of a young adult trying to figure out their financial future, I'm asking you:

Would you take 60 seconds to leave a review and help someone just like you?

Your review might be the reason a student starts saving early. It might inspire a new grad to invest wisely. It might help a young professional avoid debt traps. One small action from you can make a huge difference for someone else.

How to Leave a Review (It's Easy!):
Scan the QR code to share your thoughts.

Thank you from the bottom of my heart for paying it forward. Now, let's get back to building your secure and independent future.

- Clay Kennington

P.S. If this book helped you, consider sharing it with a friend who's ready to take control of their money. Sometimes, the best financial advice comes from someone we trust.

CHAPTER 5

HOME OWNERSHIP FOR BEGINNERS

Standing on the threshold of buying your first home is both exhilarating and daunting. The idea of owning a piece of property, a place to call entirely your own, is a powerful milestone in life's journey and the American Dream. However, it's crucial not to rush this process. Imagine the excitement of finding an incredible home; now imagine that excitement turning to overwhelming stress because you weren't financially ready. This scenario is all too common and underscores the importance of buying property when you're truly prepared. Homeownership isn't just about the joy of decorating or hosting friends for dinner; it's a significant financial commitment that can impact your life for years to come. Understanding when you're ready to take this step involves more than just having a down payment saved up; it means being financially stable and free from other burdens like substantial debt.

5.1 WHEN TO START HOME OWNERSHIP

One of the cardinal rules of home buying is to steer clear of purchasing a home while you're still in debt. Debt can significantly strain your finances, leaving little room for unexpected expenses or savings. For instance, if you're juggling student loans, credit card payments, and a car loan, adding a mortgage to the mix can quickly become too much. Homeownership carries more liability than rental contracts. When you own the home, you get to replace the water heater when it breaks. Homeowner's insurance differs from renter's insurance for substantial reasons. If you have to manage other debt on top of a mortgage, the joy of homeownership can turn into overwhelming financial burdens. Before you consider buying a home, focus on reducing or eliminating existing debts. This improves your financial health and increases your purchasing power, allowing you to secure better mortgage terms and adequate preparedness.

Another factor to consider is the stability of your living situation. Life is full of transitions, and buying a home requires a level of commitment to a particular location. If you're in a stage of life where relocations for career advancement or personal reasons are likely, it might be wise to hold off on purchasing a home. For example, consider the impact of a new job opportunity in a different city. If you've just bought a house, selling it quickly may mean losing money due to real estate market volatility or agent commissions and closing fees. Marriages often lead to similar situations, where newlyweds might need to sell their previous homes to consolidate their lives under one roof. This can lead to financial losses due to transactional costs and/or unfavorable market conditions.

To mitigate these risks, aim for at least five years of stability in your chosen location before buying a home. This period allows your property to appreciate in value, helping to offset any potential losses from market fluctuations. Real estate markets can be unpredictable, and having time on your side increases the likelihood that your investment will grow. Moreover, a longer stay provides you with the opportunity to truly understand the community, ensuring it's the right fit for your lifestyle and future plans. Stability also gives you time to save more money, which can be used for a larger down payment or unexpected home expenses, strengthening your financial position.

Our worst financial experiences have been from selling a house before the 5-year mark. Our first home was purchased at the height of a local oil boom. Three years and major improvements later, we sold for thousands of dollars in loss because the economy recessed. After a personal career setback, we sold another short-term home for only what we paid for it and had to write a check to cover commission and closing costs. Although it is inconvenient to rent, our experiences recommend delaying home purchases without a 5-year forecast.

Reflection Section: Evaluating Readiness for Homeownership

- Assess Debt Levels: List all current debts and evaluate your ability to reduce them before considering a mortgage.
- Consider Stability: Reflect on your current life stage. Are you likely to relocate for work or personal reasons in the next few years?
- Plan for the Long Term: Visualize your life in five years. Does buying a home now align with those plans?
- Financial Health Check: Ensure you have a solid emergency fund and savings beyond your down payment to handle any surprises.

These considerations form the foundation of a wise home-buying decision, ensuring that when you do take the plunge into homeownership, you do so with confidence, security, and the promise of a brighter financial future.

5.2 HOME OWNERSHIP IS INVESTING

When you think about investing, the stock market might come to mind first. However, homeownership is one of the most significant investments you can make. Unlike renting, where payments can fluctuate, owning a home stabilizes your monthly costs. Your fixed rate mortgage payment remains constant and predictable for the entire term. This shields you from the whims of the rental market and allows you to budget more effectively. Over time, this predictable monthly expense can free up resources for other financial goals, such as saving for retirement and funding a child's education. The assurance that your housing costs won't unexpectedly rise next month offers peace of mind and the ability to plan for the future without sudden surprises.

Real estate, by its nature, tends to appreciate in value over time.

While the market can experience fluctuations, the general trend over the years shows an increase in property values. This appreciation can significantly boost your net worth, turning your home into a valuable asset rather than just a place to live. Think of it as a forced savings account—each mortgage payment builds equity, which is the portion of the property you truly own. As you pay down your mortgage and property values rise, your equity increases. When you do sell, any purchase price above current mortgage value net expenses. If qualified, this sale is tax-free. Equity growth is one of the primary reasons many view homeownership as a cornerstone of building wealth. It's not just about the roof over your head; it's about the long-term financial benefits that come with owning property.

However, homeownership also comes with ongoing responsibilities that renting does not. As a homeowner, you're responsible for property taxes, maintenance, and upkeep. These aren't just minor tasks or small fees—they can be substantial and sometimes unexpected. Taxes may vary based on local government budgets and assessments, impacting your annual expenses. Maintenance is another crucial factor to consider. From leaky roofs to aging HVAC systems, repair costs can quickly add up and often come at the most inconvenient times. It's essential to budget for these expenses, setting aside a portion of your income each month into a home maintenance fund. This proactive approach ensures that when something does go wrong, you're prepared financially, and you avoid the stress of scrambling to cover costs.

Escrow accounts, often required by lenders, play a vital role in managing some of these liabilities. An escrow account is a separate account where a portion of your monthly mortgage payment is deposited to cover property taxes and homeowners insurance. This setup ensures that when these large, periodic expenses are due, the funds are readily available. While it simplifies the process, it also requires careful planning and awareness of how much is being deposited and used. Homeowners insurance is another essential expense, protecting your investment from unforeseen events like natural disasters or theft. It's crucial to review your policy annually, ensuring it provides adequate coverage for your property and belongings. While insurance and escrow might seem like mere formalities, they are integral parts of the homeownership puzzle, safeguarding your financial investment and providing peace of mind.

5.3 HOW MUCH HOUSE CAN YOU AFFORD?

Picture yourself standing outside a charming house, imagining the life you could build within its walls. The excitement is palpable, yet it's critical to ground that dream in financial reality. The allure of purchasing a home can lead many to stretch their budgets, but the consequences of overextending financially can be burdensome. When you approach a bank for a mortgage, they might present you with a loan amount that seems generous, perhaps even flattering. It's tempting to think, "If the bank says I can afford it, it must be true." However, banks often use formulas that might not consider your individual needs, personal goals, lifestyle choices, or unforeseen expenses. Their business is to increase their portfolios. They base their calculations on general criteria that might not align with your specific circumstances or long-term plans.

Instead of relying solely on what a bank offers, consider what feels comfortable for you. A good rule of thumb is to keep your monthly mortgage payment within 25% of your total budget. This basis allows you to manage your housing costs without sacrificing other financial obligations or lifestyle desires. It leaves room for savings, investments, and the occasional splurge on things that bring joy and enrichment to your life. Living within this margin ensures that you can comfortably handle your mortgage alongside other expenses like groceries, utilities, and transportation, without constantly feeling financially stretched. This balance is crucial for maintaining peace of mind and financial stability, allowing you to enjoy your home without the constant worry of making ends meet.

Another key factor in determining how much house you can afford is the down payment. The more you can put down upfront, the better. A substantial down payment reduces the loan amount, thus lowering your monthly payments and the total interest paid over the life of the loan. It also increases your equity from the start, giving you a stronger financial stake in the property. Additionally, a larger down payment might eliminate the need for private mortgage insurance (PMI), which lenders typically require if you put down less than 20%. PMI can add a significant cost to your monthly payments, so avoiding it can save you a considerable amount of money in the long term. PMI does not protect you; banking practices force you to pay it to protect them.

Paying off your mortgage quickly is important. While a traditional 30-year mortgage offers lower monthly payments, it also means paying more interest over time. Consider the difference in opting for a 15-year mortgage. These options usually come with lower interest rates and enable you to build equity faster. Regardless of your mortgage term, making extra payments toward the principal can significantly reduce the loan duration and the total interest paid. This approach requires discipline and planning, but the financial freedom gained from owning your home outright is well worth the effort.

When assessing how much house you can afford, it's also important to consider the broader picture of homeownership costs. Beyond the mortgage, you'll need to account for property taxes, insurance, maintenance, and potential homeowner association fees. These expenses can vary widely depending on politics, location, property size, and age. Researching these costs in advance helps prevent unwelcome surprises and ensures your budget reflects the true cost of homeownership. By taking a comprehensive view of these factors, you empower yourself to make informed decisions that align with your financial goals and provide a stable foundation for your future.

Buying a home is a significant financial decision, one that requires careful consideration and planning. It's about finding the right balance between your dreams and your budget, ensuring that your home is not only a place of comfort and joy but also a wise investment in your future. As you navigate this process, remember that the goal is not just to buy a house but to secure a home that supports your lifestyle and aspirations without compromising your financial health.

5.4 TIPS FOR FIRST-TIME HOMEBUYERS

Navigating the world of home buying for the first time can feel like entering a maze without a map. The process is filled with excitement and the potential for missteps. One of the most critical elements of real estate is location. Where you choose to live impacts not only your daily life but also your home's future value. Begin by researching neighborhoods that fit your lifestyle and needs. Consider factors like proximity to work, schools, public transportation, and amenities. Dive into local market trends to understand how property values have shifted over the years. This insight can help you identify areas with growth potential, ensuring your investment appreciates over time. Location isn't just about the physical space; it's about the community you'll become part of and the lifestyle you'll lead.

Once you've honed in on a location, securing a trustworthy real estate agent becomes paramount. A good agent is more than just a salesperson; they are your guide through the complexities of buying a home. Start by seeking recommendations from friends and family, then interview multiple agents to find one whose values align with yours. Discuss your priorities and budget openly; agents are obligated to act in your best interest. A transparent relationship ensures your agent can advocate effectively on your behalf. They should understand the financial aspects and your needs and vision for your new home. An agent who truly listens will help you find properties that meet your criteria and negotiate the best deal possible. Remember, your agent is your partner in this process, so choose someone you feel comfortable communicating with and who genuinely has your best interests at heart.

Before you start visiting potential homes, it's wise to become prequalified for a mortgage. Prequalification starts your relationship with the bank and gives you a clear picture of what you can afford. This makes the home search more focused and efficient. It also strengthens your position in the eyes of sellers, as it demonstrates that you're serious and financially capable. The process involves providing your lender with basic financial information, such as your income, assets, and debts. In return, you'll receive an estimate of the loan amount you might qualify for. This step isn't binding but serves as a valuable guide. With a prequalification letter in hand, you can confidently explore homes within your budget, avoiding the heartbreak of falling in love with a property that is financially out of reach.

As you tour potential homes, keep an eye out for opportunities to add value. This doesn't mean seeking out properties in disrepair but rather identifying homes with features that can be enhanced or updated over time. Perhaps a house with an unfinished basement could be transformed into living space. Find a yard that could benefit from landscaping. The best value may be found in the ugliest house in the neighborhood, especially if it needs a little inexpensive TLC. As what makes the house ugly can be transformed, seek vision as you shop. Improvements can increase your enjoyment of the home and boost its resale value. When evaluating properties, think about both your current needs and future possibilities. A home with room to grow can adapt to life changes, making it a long-term investment. Consider how updates might align with your skills and interests—whether you're handy with tools or prefer to hire professionals, knowing your limits will help you make informed decisions.

Throughout the home buying process, remain open to learning and adapting. The real estate market is dynamic, and new opportunities arise frequently. Stay informed by reading market reports and attending open houses, even if you're not ready to make an offer. This practice keeps you attuned to pricing and trends, sharpening your instincts as a buyer. Additionally, consider taking a home buying workshop or consulting with a financial advisor to deepen your understanding. The more knowledge you gather, the more empowered you'll feel in making decisions that align with your goals. Home buying is a multi-faceted experience, blending emotion with practicality, and finding the right balance is key to a successful purchase.

5.5 REAL ESTATE INVESTING EXAMPLES

Understanding the dynamics of real estate can often feel abstract until you hear about real people who have navigated these waters. Let me share a couple of stories that highlight both the triumphs and lessons learned in the world of property investment and first-time home buying. These stories aren't just about the figures or the properties themselves; they're about the individuals who dared to take the plunge, each with their own set of challenges and ambitions.

Meet Jason, a young real estate investor who saw potential where others saw risk. In his early twenties, Jason recognized the growing demand for rental properties in his college town. With a modest savings and a keen eye for opportunity, he purchased a small duplex. The property needed some work, but the location was ideal for student rentals. Jason spent weekends repairing and upgrading the units, learning as he went. His willingness to roll up his sleeves and get involved turned out to be a smart move. Within a year, both units were rented, providing a steady income stream that covered the mortgage and left him with extra cash to reinvest. By his late twenties, Jason had expanded his portfolio to include several properties, all strategically located in high-demand areas. His story illustrates that with research, patience, and a bit of elbow grease, real estate can be a lucrative investment even for those just starting out. Jason's approach was not about chasing quick returns but focusing on sustainable growth and long-term value.

Emily and Mark were married and decided it was time to buy their first home. They had always rented and felt ready to invest in a place of their own. They began the process with high hopes, dreaming of a charming bungalow in a friendly neighborhood. However, their journey wasn't as straightforward as they had anticipated. The housing market in their area was competitive, with homes selling above asking price. Their initial offers on two homes fell through, leaving them disheartened. But instead of giving up, Emily and Mark took each setback as a lesson. They realized the importance of being pre-approved for a mortgage and adjusting their budget expectations. They also learned to act quickly when a suitable property hit the market. Finally, they found a cozy home that ticked most of their boxes, and with their newfound knowledge, they successfully negotiated a fair price. The experience taught them the value of resilience and adaptability in the home-buying process. They discovered that being prepared, flexible, and informed made all the difference in achieving their dream.

For first-time buyers like Emily and Mark, the journey to homeownership can be filled with unexpected twists. Yet, each experience, whether a misstep or a victory, offers invaluable insights. It's essential to approach the process with an open mind, ready to learn and adapt. Real estate investment and home buying are not just about the financial stakes but also about understanding and navigating the human elements involved. The experiences of both Jason and the newlyweds highlight the need for patience, research, and a willingness to learn from each situation.

These examples demonstrate that real estate, whether for investment or personal use, involves more than numbers on a ledger. It's about people with aspirations and the courage to pursue them. Each decision, each lesson learned, adds to the story of your financial journey, shaping you not just as a homeowner or investor but as someone who actively participates in creating their future. As you consider your next steps in real estate, let these stories inspire you to see beyond the challenges and focus on the possibilities that lie ahead.

5.6 FIX UP A FIXER UPPER

Imagine walking through a house that's seen better days: chipped paint, outdated fixtures, and a garden overtaken by weeds. To some, this might look like a daunting project, but to others, it's a canvas brimming with potential. Buying a fixer-upper isn't just about acquiring property; it's about embracing the opportunity to breathe new life into a space. The journey of transforming a fixer-upper into a home adds value to the property and offers you the chance to learn valuable skills that extend beyond mere construction. The same principles of successful real estate still apply, so do your homework and make a wise financial investment.

Taking on a fixer-upper quickly becomes a learning experience. As you tackle each project, you gain hands-on skills in areas like carpentry, plumbing, and even electrical work. There are so many resources to utilize in learning these tasks in today's digital age. These are skills that stay with you, allowing for future home improvements without the hefty price tag of hiring a professional. You might start small, painting walls or replacing fixtures, and gradually move on to larger projects, like installing new flooring. Each completed task not only enhances the home but also boosts your confidence and competence. The knowledge gained can be applied to future homes or even shared with friends and family, turning you into a valuable resource within your community.

Collaboration is another rewarding aspect of fixing up a home. Friends and family can become invaluable allies in your renovation endeavors. Working together makes the tasks more manageable and transforms them into opportunities for bonding and shared achievement. Picture a weekend where everyone gathers to repaint rooms or plant new flowers in the garden. These collaborative efforts turn work into fun, creating memories that last well beyond the project's completion. Plus, sharing skills and ideas can lead to innovative solutions you might not have considered on your own. For instance, a friend with a knack for design might help you envision a layout you hadn't thought possible, while another with carpentry skills can assist with building custom shelving. These partnerships can transform what might seem like a daunting solo project into an enjoyable group activity.

The satisfaction of completing a fixer-upper goes beyond the physical transformation. It's about the sense of accomplishment that comes from overcoming challenges and creating a space that reflects your vision and hard work. Each room renovated becomes a testament to your perseverance and creativity. This sense of ownership and pride in your home is deeply fulfilling, knowing that you've played a direct role in shaping it. The process also instills a deeper appreciation for your living space, having invested time and effort into making it truly yours. This emotional connection can make the house feel more like home, a place filled with your personal touches and memories.

The financial benefits of renovating a fixer-upper can be significant. By purchasing a property below-market value and investing in improvements, you can increase its worth substantially. This may lead to a higher return on investment when you decide to sell in the future. The ability to enhance your financial position while simultaneously creating a home you love is a compelling reason to consider taking on a fixer-upper.

If you consider a fixer-upper, remember that it's not just about the end product but the journey of transformation and growth. You'll learn new skills, forge stronger connections with those who help you, and create a home that reflects your efforts and style. It adds confidence to enjoy the beauty and functionality in what you create. It's an adventure that offers both personal and financial rewards, shaping not just your living space but also your capabilities and confidence as a homeowner.

Chapter 5 has explored the multifaceted world of homeownership, from determining readiness to embracing the transformative potential of fixer-uppers. These insights lay the groundwork for making informed decisions, empowering you to navigate the real estate landscape with confidence and clarity. As we transition into Chapter 6, we'll delve into navigating educational choices, uncovering how strategic decisions in furthering education can also fortify your financial foundation.

CHAPTER 6
NAVIGATING EDUCATION CHOICES

Imagine standing on the cusp of your college journey, a world of opportunities stretching before you. The excitement is palpable, but so are the questions buzzing in your mind. Which degree should you pursue? Will it lead to a fulfilling career? More importantly, will it provide a return on investment (ROI) that justifies the cost? In today's rapidly evolving job market, evaluating the ROI of your education can guide you toward informed choices that align with both your passions and financial goals. Just as you wouldn't buy a car without considering its long-term value, approaching your education with a similar mindset ensures that your investment yields rewarding dividends over time.

6.1 EDUCATION RETURN ON INVESTMENT

The concept of ROI in education is about assessing the potential financial return a degree offers relative to its cost in both money and time. It's a practical tool to weigh the benefits against the expenses, helping you make decisions that support your future stability. Over the last few years, education costs have increased greatly, leaving some graduates questioning their chosen industry. Degrees in engineering or healthcare, however, offer some of the best ROIs for graduates, thanks to high-demand and competitive salaries. The median monthly earnings for engineering degree holders can reach impressive figures, highlighting the financial viability of such paths. In contrast, degrees with lower earning potential might require careful consideration to ensure they align with your career aspirations and financial situation.

Several factors influence the educational ROI, especially the chosen field of study and the associated job market. Some degrees generally lead to high-paying positions due to the specialized skills they impart. The job market's demand for these skills ensures that graduates find ample opportunities for employment and advancement. For example, healthcare professions are growing rapidly. They are driven by an aging population and a shortage of medical professionals (Source 1). Understanding these dynamics can help you select a degree that aligns with your interests and offers robust employment prospects. Graduate employability rates also play a crucial role. Degrees with higher employability rates tend to deliver better ROI, as graduates can secure jobs more quickly and start earning sooner.

To assist in assessing educational ROI, several tools are available that provide insights into the financial benefits of various degrees. Online ROI calculators, for instance, allow you to input different parameters, such as tuition costs and potential earnings, to compare the financial outcomes of multiple educational paths. These calculators can illuminate the long-term value of a degree, helping you make informed choices. Additionally, examining case studies of graduates from different fields can offer real-world perspectives. Reading about someone who pursued a degree in electrical engineering and quickly advanced to a high-earning position provides concrete evidence of the potential ROI. On the flip side, learning about someone who struggled in a less lucrative field can offer cautionary tales that guide your decision-making process.

Maximizing the ROI of your chosen degree involves strategic actions beyond just selecting the right field. Networking and internships are invaluable for career advancement, providing hands-on experience and connections that can open doors to job opportunities. Engaging with professionals in your desired field, attending industry events, and seeking mentorship can all contribute to building a strong professional network. Continuing education and certifications further enhance your credentials, making you more competitive in the job market. These additional qualifications demonstrate a commitment to your field and can lead to higher earning potential and career advancement. By actively pursuing these opportunities, you position yourself to maximize the financial return on your educational investment, ensuring that your degree serves as a solid foundation for future success.

Reflection Section

- Evaluate: Utilize an online ROI calculator to compare potential earnings across different fields you're considering.
- Research: Explore case studies of graduates in your desired field to understand their career paths and ROI.
- Plan: Identify networking events or internships in your area that can provide valuable industry connections.

6.2 CHOOSING AN AFFORDABLE COLLEGE EXPERIENCE

The weight of college tuition can feel overwhelming, making the dream of higher education seem financially daunting. Yet, there are strategic ways to ease this burden and make college more affordable. One practical approach is starting your education at a community college before transferring to a university. This path offers a cost-effective solution, as community colleges typically charge significantly lower tuition rates than four-year institutions. For example, completing your general education requirements at a community college can save you thousands of dollars, which you can then allocate towards your major courses at a university. Additionally, many community colleges have established transfer agreements with local universities, ensuring that the credits you earn will count toward your degree. This seamless transition allows you to enjoy the benefits of a university education without the hefty price tag from the start.

Scholarships and grants are another crucial avenue for reducing educational expenses. Unlike loans, these funds do not require repayment, making them a valuable resource for students seeking financial relief. Scholarships are available from various sources, including schools, private organizations, and local community groups. Applying for scholarships may seem time-consuming, but the potential payoff is well worth the effort. Even if the expected success rate is low, applying to many scholarships can be a great use of your time. If you spend 100 hours applying and receive $5000, your investment calculates to $50 per hour. You won't get that at minimum wage jobs! Grants, often based on financial need, provide additional support and can significantly lower the cost of attending college. By dedicating time to research and apply for these opportunities, you can lessen your dependence on student loans and reduce long-term debt. See the last subsection of this chapter to become expert in getting scholarships.

Attending a local college or university offers another layer of cost savings through in-state tuition. In-state tuition rates are generally much lower than out-of-state rates, often making a significant difference in your overall college expenses. This difference is due to the subsidies provided by state governments, which aim to make higher education more accessible to residents. By choosing a school close to home, you not only save on tuition but also on additional costs like housing and travel. Living at home during college can cut expenses drastically, freeing up funds for other priorities or reducing the need for loans. Exploring in-state options can provide a quality education while keeping your financial future intact.

When selecting a college, it's crucial to consider institutions that offer value for money. Evaluating schools based on academic heritage or football success may lead to unfortunate outcomes. The degree and institution will matter much more to you than hiring professionals: they will only care that you are prepared to do the job skills. A college with a strong reputation and successful graduates is likely to offer valuable networking opportunities and career support. In the end, however, you will be responsible for marketing yourself and preparing for great opportunities. That can be done at nearly any institution. Visiting campuses and attending information sessions can give you a feel for the environment and resources available. Talking to current students and faculty can provide firsthand insights into the academic experience and campus life, helping you make an informed decision that aligns with both your educational and financial goals.

Personal stories of students who have successfully managed college expenses can offer both inspiration and practical tips. Take, for instance, Emma, who started her college journey at a community college, covering almost all of her tuition with local scholarships. Her frugality and diligence allowed her to transfer to a state university without any debt. Another example is Jack, who chose to attend his local university while living at home. By doing so, he saved significantly on living expenses and graduated debt-free, ready to enter the workforce unburdened by financial stress. These narratives demonstrate that with careful planning and strategic choices, you can pursue higher education without compromising your financial future.

6.3 BALANCING EDUCATION WITH FINANCIAL REALITIES

College life is often a juggling act between education and finances, a reality faced by countless students. Many balance part-time work alongside their studies, a necessity for covering tuition, books, and daily expenses. This dual commitment can be taxing, as it requires meticulous time management and energy allocation. Imagine rushing from a lecture to a job, only to return home late, exhausted, with assignments still waiting. It's a common narrative, yet one that highlights the resilience and determination of students striving to achieve their goals.

Maintaining financial health during your college years involves practical strategies tailored to your unique situation. Many student loans actually fund elevated living expenses of college, not tuition. Budgeting becomes a crucial tool, helping you allocate funds wisely and avoid unnecessary debt. Crafting a budget involves listing all income sources, such as part-time jobs or financial aid, and tracking expenses, from rent to groceries and semester tuition. By identifying essential costs and potential savings, you can create a financial plan that accommodates both your needs and your academic commitments. Additionally, taking advantage of student discounts and resources can significantly ease financial pressures. Many local businesses offer discounts to students, while campuses often provide free or low-cost services, such as gym memberships and public transportation passes. Utilizing these resources allows you to stretch your budget further, ensuring you maintain a healthy financial balance without compromising your educational experience.

Strategic financial planning plays a pivotal role in educational success, offering a framework to manage both immediate and long-term financial responsibilities. Creating a comprehensive financial plan for the duration of your studies involves setting clear goals and timelines. This plan should include projections of expected income and expenses, as well as savings targets for emergencies or unforeseen costs. By planning ahead, you can anticipate challenges and make informed decisions that align with your academic objectives. Colleges can generally forecast details of costs associated with each semester of your degree. It then becomes critically important that you stick to that schedule by passing each of your classes and staying on target to complete a 4-year degree in 8 semesters.

Consider the stories of students who have successfully balanced education and finances, illustrating the power of determination and strategic planning. Take Sarah, a full-time student who worked evenings at a local café to support herself. Despite the demanding schedule, she managed to excel academically by meticulously organizing her time and prioritizing tasks. She also discovered a few hours and rotations that blessed her with significantly better tips at the cafe. Her experience taught her the value of discipline and adaptability, skills that would later benefit her career. Then there's Daniel, who faced significant financial challenges during his studies. By leveraging on-campus resources, applying for scholarships, and embracing a frugal lifestyle, he minimized his debt and graduated with honors. His journey highlights the importance of resourcefulness and resilience, demonstrating that financial hardships can be overcome with the right mindset and tools. These narratives underscore the diverse paths students take to achieve their educational aspirations, offering inspiration and practical insights for managing both academic and financial demands.

6.4 SPEED OF CASH: CONTINUE STUDYING ONLY AS FAST AS YOU CAN PAY FOR IT

Picture yourself at the crossroads of education and finance, where many students stand pondering their next steps. The prospect of continuing your studies without accumulating debt is not only appealing but also attainable if approached with a strategy that aligns with the rhythm of your finances. One effective way to manage this is to study only as fast as you can pay for it. This approach might mean taking break years to gain work experience, which enriches your resume and allows you to save up for the remaining tuition. Internships during these breaks can provide invaluable insights into your field of study, giving you a competitive edge once you return to your academic pursuits. Moreover, the work experience gained can often translate into higher starting salaries after graduation, further validating the time spent outside the classroom.

Summer jobs and side hustles present another avenue to bolster your financial position while studying. These opportunities often align with the gig economy, allowing you to balance work with academic commitments. Many students have discovered that their creative side hustles not only provide financial support but also open doors to unexpected career paths. Whether it's freelancing in graphic design, tutoring, or developing apps, the skills and networks you build can be more lucrative than anticipated. Consider the story of Jake, who started a side hustle as a photographer while studying. When a college landlord needed help fixing apartments, Billy became his primary handyman on-call for a significant dollar-per-hour arrangement. What began as hobbies turned into thriving businesses, enabling these two to cover tuition costs and graduate debt-free. Their success exemplifies how leveraging your talents and interests can transform financial constraints into opportunities for growth and learning.

While I was in college, a graduating classmate offered me her part-time job. She had worked several years at a local engineering firm. For the remaining semesters, I gained a salary and invaluable professional experience that boosted my resume qualifications for my developing career.

Exploring tuition reimbursement programs can further support your educational endeavors. Many employers offer these programs as part of their benefits package, providing financial assistance for tuition in exchange for your commitment to the company. This arrangement not only reduces the immediate financial burden of education but also solidifies your relationship with an employer who values your development. Research companies that offer such benefits to be a strategic move, especially if you're considering work while studying. By aligning your employment with tuition reimbursement opportunities, you ensure that your job directly contributes to your educational goals. This synergy between work and study enhances your financial stability and fosters a sense of purpose, knowing that your efforts are tangibly supporting your academic progress.

Working creatively within the gig economy or through internships can yield financial benefits that extend beyond mere income. The skills honed, the networks built, and the experiences gained enrich your personal and professional life, often in ways a traditional classroom setting cannot. Consider the narrative of Lisa, who spent her summers developing a digital marketing side hustle. Her initiative funded her education and positioned her as a sought-after candidate post-graduation, with several companies vying for her expertise. Stories like Lisa's remind us that the path to education isn't always linear. By leveraging the flexibility of the gig economy and understanding the value of work experience, you create a dynamic educational experience that is as financially sustainable as it is enriching.

6.5 COLLEGE MAJOR SELECTION

Deciding on a college major is like choosing a direction for the next chapter of your life. It's a decision that carries weight, both intellectually and financially. Yet, many students find themselves plunging into a major without fully understanding what it entails or where it might lead them. This lack of clarity can lead to wasted time and money if you realize later that the chosen path doesn't align with your true interests or career goals. Before committing, allow yourself the space to explore various subjects and interests. If you're unsure about what you want to pursue, consider taking general education courses first. They offer a broader perspective on different fields, helping you identify what truly resonates with you. Should you decide to switch majors, do so with careful thought and purpose. Switching isn't just about starting anew; it's about aligning your education with your evolving interests and goals, ensuring that your time and financial investment lead to fulfilling outcomes.

When selecting a major, it's crucial to consider the practical implications of your choice. Study job placement rates in your field of interest to gauge the likelihood of post-graduation employment. Some fields boast high placement rates and lucrative salaries, while others may offer less stability. Also, consider where those specific jobs are located. Understanding these trends helps you make informed decisions about whether a particular major aligns with your long-term goals. Additionally, look beyond the classroom to see how college coursework translates to real-world application. Consider whether the skills and knowledge you'll acquire in your major are in demand in the job market. This foresight can prevent the frustration of completing a degree only to find limited job opportunities. Engage with academic advisors and career counselors who can provide insights into how different majors connect to various industries and career paths, ensuring that your education lays a solid foundation for your future.

Networking is an invaluable tool when it comes to selecting and succeeding in a major. Professional organizations related to your field of interest offer networking opportunities, industry insights, and potential job leads. Joining such organizations as a student provides a head start, connecting you with professionals who can offer guidance and mentorship. Attend events, workshops, and conferences to build relationships with individuals working in your desired field. These connections can provide insider knowledge about industry trends and expectations, giving you a competitive edge. Additionally, engaging with alumni networks can offer valuable insights into the career outcomes of graduates from your chosen major. Alumni can share first-hand experiences of how their education prepared them for the work-force and offer advice on navigating the transition from college to career.

As you navigate the process of choosing a major, consider the story of a student who initially pursued a degree in biology, driven by a passion for the environment. However, after taking several courses, they realized that their true interest lay in environmental policy rather than science. By switching to a major in environmental studies with a policy focus, they aligned their academic pursuits with their career goals. This decision, though initially daunting, ultimately led to a fulfilling career in environmental advocacy. Their story highlights the importance of remaining open to change and ensuring that your major reflects your true interests and aspirations.

Choosing a major is about more than just academic interest; it's about aligning your education with your personal and professional aspirations. By taking the time to understand the implications of your choice, you ensure that your college experience supports your career goals and sets you on a path to success.

6.6 BECOME EXPERT IN GETTING SCHOLARSHIPS

In the realm of funding education, scholarships are often the unsung heroes, quietly offering sizable support to those who know where to look and how to apply. Each year, thousands of dollars in scholarships remain unclaimed simply because students don't apply. You might think the competition is too fierce or that you don't stand a chance, but here's the secret: persistence pays off. Even with acceptance rates hovering below 10%, the potential reward is significant. You're not just applying for monetary assistance; you're investing in yourself, and the return on this investment can be immense. When you consider the time spent compared to the potential financial gain, the hourly rate can outshine many part-time jobs.

To set yourself apart, leverage your community involvement. Many scholarships are awarded based on more than just academic achievements; they consider your contributions to your community and how you've made an impact. Volunteer work, leadership roles, and participation in local events can all strengthen your application. Scholarship committees love to see applicants who are actively engaged and making a difference. This involvement enriches your life experience and builds a compelling narrative for your applications. So, tap into local organizations, clubs, or volunteer groups. Your community is a rich resource for opportunities that can bolster your scholarship applications.

Understanding the scholarship landscape is crucial. Scholarships can come from various sources: local businesses, religious organizations, civic groups, and professional associations. Each has its criteria and focus areas, so doing your homework is vital. Research these opportunities thoroughly. Many platforms and websites aggregate scholarships, providing a starting point for your search. Don't overlook smaller, local scholarships; they often have less competition than national ones, increasing your chances of success. Your high school or college guidance counselor can also be a valuable resource in identifying local opportunities tailored to your background and interests.

When applying, treat each scholarship application like a job application. Tailor your responses to fit the specific criteria and goals of the scholarship. If an essay is required, approach it as an opportunity to tell your story. Highlight your achievements, challenges overcome, and future aspirations. Make your application stand out by showcasing your unique perspective and experiences. Reuse essays when possible, tweaking them to fit each application's requirements. This saves time and allows you to refine your narrative with each submission. Remember, scholarship providers want to invest in individuals who demonstrate potential, passion, and a commitment to their goals.

Persistence is key. Apply to as many scholarships as possible, even those you think are a long shot. The more you apply, the greater your chances of receiving financial gifts. Keep an organized system to track deadlines and requirements, ensuring you never miss an opportunity. And don't get discouraged by rejections; they're part of the process. Each application is a step closer to securing funding, and the experience gained from each submission can improve future applications. Additionally, maintain a positive online presence, as many scholarship committees may review your social media profiles to get a sense of your character and background.

Scholarships are not just financial lifelines; they're affirmations of your hard work and potential. By approaching them with strategy and dedication, you can significantly reduce the financial burden of your education, allowing you to focus on what truly matters: learning and growing. As you master the art of scholarship applications, you're not only securing financial aid but also building skills in self-presentation and perseverance that will benefit you throughout your career and life.

As we conclude this chapter, remember that education is a multifaceted journey, enriched by the choices and strategies you employ. From selecting the right major to securing scholarships, each decision shapes your path. Looking ahead, we'll explore career growth, examining how your education choices intersect with professional opportunities.

CHAPTER 7
NAVIGATING CAREER DECISIONS

Picture this: you're sipping your morning beverage, scrolling through job listings, overwhelmed by the sheer volume of options and possibilities. The career landscape today is a vast ocean, teeming with new roles and opportunities that our parents' generation could hardly have imagined. Gone are the days when a single career path defined your entire working life. Now, flexibility and adaptability are the keys to thriving in a world where technology and innovation continuously reshape the job market. The notion of settling into a single job for decades has become obsolete, replaced by the exciting, albeit daunting, prospect of crafting a career that evolves with your values and aspirations.

7.1 USE CAREER TO FULFILL PERSONAL PURPOSE

In this dynamic environment, your career should be more than just a paycheck; it should be a reflection of your personal values and a path to fulfillment. It may be all about the opportunities available to you. A major shift is evident in movements like the Great Resignation, where individuals seek roles that resonate with their values and offer genuine satisfaction. The idea is simple yet profound: your job should excite you, leverage your strengths, and allow you to do what you love. This alignment not only boosts job satisfaction but also enhances performance and retention, as noted in various studies on employee engagement.

To achieve this alignment, begin by identifying your core values. Consider what drives you, the issues that ignite your passion, and the environments where you thrive. Self-reflection is crucial in this process. Ask yourself what aspects of your previous jobs brought you joy and which ones drained your energy. Once you clearly understand your values, use them as a compass to guide your career decisions. When evaluating job opportunities, assess whether potential employers share these values and provide a culture that supports them. During job interviews, pose questions that help you gauge this alignment, and pay attention to your gut feeling about the company's ethos and practices.

Starting at the highest job possible is a practical tip as you navigate your career. This doesn't necessarily mean aiming for the top position immediately but rather seeking roles that challenge you and propel you toward your long-term goals. By aiming high, you place yourself in environments that foster growth and learning. However, avoid the paralysis that can come from overthinking every decision. Often, the best way to discover your path is to get started somewhere. Even if the job isn't your dream role, the experience you gain will be invaluable, and it might lead to unexpected opportunities or insights about what you truly want.

Once you're in the workforce, brainstorming and strategizing about your career trajectory is essential. Take the time to map out where you are now and where you want to be in the future. Consider the skills and experiences you need to acquire to bridge this gap. Set clear, actionable steps to achieve these milestones, and regularly revisit your plan to ensure it remains aligned with your evolving interests and the ever-changing job market. Be assertive in exploring other employment options and learning about new fields. Attend industry events, workshops, and seminars to broaden your horizon and network with professionals who might offer guidance or mentorship. This proactive approach keeps you informed about the trends and opportunities that align with your purpose, enabling you to make informed and intentional career decisions.

At the heart of this journey is the understanding that your career is a living entity, capable of growth and change. Embrace the fluidity of modern work life as an opportunity to continuously refine your path, ensuring it always reflects your personal purpose and aspirations. Use every role, every challenge, and every success as a stepping stone toward a career that sustains you financially and fulfills you on a deeply personal level.

7.2 NETWORK MENTORS TO DISCOVER POSSIBILITIES

Imagine you're at a crossroads in your career, unsure of which path to take. One of the most powerful tools you have at your disposal is mentorship. A mentor isn't just someone who's been in the industry longer; they're a guide who can help illuminate the paths you might not have considered. Networking with mentors opens doors to new opportunities and insights that can transform your career trajectory. Start by looking within your current organization. The corporate ladder isn't just a cliché; it's a framework that can offer you a wealth of learning opportunities. Engage with senior colleagues who have navigated the same paths you're considering. Their experiences can provide valuable lessons and strategies that textbooks simply can't.

But don't limit yourself to your immediate environment. The world is vast, and so are the career possibilities. Many are recruited to new jobs from friends or even friends of friends. Everyone around you and around them can be invaluable resources in your quest for career growth. These interactions can reveal the nuances of different fields, helping you make informed decisions about your next steps.

Exploring the corporate ladder doesn't mean you have to climb it in the traditional sense. It's about understanding the structure and opportunities within your organization and how they align with your career goals. Start by reviewing your company's organizational chart and identifying departments or roles that pique your interest. Arrange informational interviews with individuals in those roles to gain insights into their daily responsibilities and the skills required. This proactive approach allows you to tailor your skill development to meet the demands of your desired position, increasing your chances of success when opportunities arise.

Networking isn't just about meeting new people; it's about nurturing relationships that can support you throughout your career. Building these connections requires effort and intention. Participate in industry-specific events, join professional groups, and engage in community activities that align with your interests. These settings provide opportunities to meet like-minded individuals who share your passions and can become part of your professional network. When engaging with new contacts, approach conversations with genuine curiosity, a willingness to learn and also to give back. Ask insightful questions and listen actively, showing respect for their expertise and experiences.

To find a different job, utilize a combination of networking and mentorship. Ask friends and family whom they know that works in the preferred field or company. Ask for an introduction and a few minutes with the those contacts to discuss future opportunities. Interview these new contacts on what they see as potential needs, what they like about working there and how you could prepare. Interview as many people as possible with simple introductions. Thank not only your friends but also the new contacts for their information.

7.3 RECOGNIZE CHANGING TRENDS AND EMERGING OPPORTUNITIES

In the rapidly evolving landscape of today's workforce, technology is not just a tool; it's a catalyst for transformation across every industry. Whether you're in healthcare, finance, education, or even agriculture, technological advancements are reshaping how we work, communicate, and innovate. The pace of change is staggering, and keeping up can feel like trying to catch a speeding train. But within this whirlwind lies opportunity, especially for those who are willing to adapt and embrace the new possibilities that technology brings. Being attuned to these changes isn't just about survival; it's about positioning yourself for success in a future where the only constant is change.

Creativity and flexibility have become indispensable skills in navigating this dynamic environment. New technologies are constantly emerging, and with them come fresh career paths and roles that were unimaginable a decade ago. Think about the rise of artificial intelligence, blockchain, and virtual reality; each of these fields has spawned numerous jobs that didn't exist before. To stay ahead, you'll need to cultivate a mindset that is open to learning and experimentation. Regularly updating your skill set and staying informed about industry trends will allow you to pivot and seize opportunities as they arise. This might mean diving into podcasts, attending tech conferences, or joining professional groups that focus on emerging technologies. By doing so, you position yourself not only to respond to changes but to anticipate and leverage them for your career growth.

Producing online content related to your passions is a powerful way to engage with these emerging trends and showcase your adaptability. In today's digital age, the internet is a vast platform that offers endless possibilities for sharing your expertise and creativity with a global audience. Whether it's blogging about industry insights, creating video tutorials on YouTube, or posting thought-provoking articles on LinkedIn, producing content allows you to build a personal brand and establish yourself as an authority in your field. This visibility can open doors to new opportunities, such as collaborations, job offers, or even invitations to speak at industry events. Moreover, the process of creating content forces you to stay current with trends and continuously refine your skills, keeping you sharp and relevant in a competitive job market. The world would be a better place if everyone produced some kind of positive content.

Consider the story of Alex, a graphic designer who was passionate about digital art and animation. By starting a YouTube channel where he shared tutorials and industry news, Alex honed his skills and attracted a following of like-minded individuals. This platform became a springboard for his career, leading to freelance projects, consulting opportunities, and eventually a full-time role with a tech company that valued his innovative approach and digital presence. Alex's journey highlights the power of producing content and how it can transform a passion into professional success. It also underscores the importance of being proactive and taking initiative, even when the path isn't clearly defined.

The beauty of this approach is that it allows you to blend your personal interests with professional growth. Whatever your passion—be it technology, sustainability, or culinary arts—there's a niche waiting for you to explore and influence. The digital world is vast and varied, and there's space for every voice. By sharing your insights and perspectives, you not only contribute to your field but also expand your network and influence. And as you engage with your audience, you receive feedback and ideas that can further your development and inspire new directions. This cycle of creation and interaction fosters a more profound understanding of your industry and keeps you at the forefront of innovation.

As the landscape of work continues to shift, recognizing and adapting to emerging trends is not just advantageous; it's necessary. Embrace the changes, stay informed, and remain curious. By doing so, you will not only navigate the challenges of a tech-driven world but thrive within it, crafting a dynamic career as exciting as the era we live in.

7.4 CRAFTING A CAREER THAT FITS YOUR CALLING

Imagine waking up each day excited about the work ahead, knowing it aligns with your deepest values and interests. This is not a fantasy but a realistic goal when you prioritize personal fulfillment in your career choices. Career satisfaction often hinges on aligning your job with your core values and interests—those principles that drive your actions and define who you are. To identify these, consider moments when you felt most energized and engaged. Was it when helping others, solving complex problems, or perhaps when being creative? Once you recognize these values, you can use them as a compass in your career decisions, ensuring that each step you take aligns with what truly matters to you.

Discovering a fulfilling career path requires a blend of introspection and exploration. Begin by conducting informational interviews, which are informal conversations with professionals in fields that pique your interest. These discussions provide insights into daily responsibilities, industry challenges, and potential career trajectories, offering a realistic glimpse into different roles. Career assessments, such as aptitude tests or personality profiles, can also help uncover paths that align with your strengths and preferences. These tools provide a structured framework for evaluating options, helping you make informed decisions about your future. Additionally, consider volunteering or taking on part-time roles in fields that intrigue you. These experiences offer hands-on exposure and can confirm whether a particular path resonates with your values and interests.

Pursuing a career aligned with your calling offers numerous benefits. Firstly, it enhances job satisfaction and motivation. When your work reflects your passions, you approach tasks with enthusiasm and commitment, making it easier to navigate challenges. This alignment also fosters greater resilience. When faced with setbacks, knowing that your work contributes to something meaningful can provide the strength to persevere. Furthermore, a career that aligns with your calling can lead to both personal and professional success. It encourages continuous learning and growth, as you're more likely to seek opportunities that expand your skills and knowledge in areas that excite you. This not only benefits your career progression but also enriches your personal life, as the fulfillment you gain from your work spills over into other aspects of your existence.

In a conversation with Chad, a soon-to-be college graduate, his aspiration to become a high school teacher and coach was evident. He expressed concerns about the financial prospects of such a career. Together, we delved into the surprising findings of studies on wealth accumulation, which reveal that teaching is the third most common profession among millionaires in the United States. This revelation highlighted how strategic financial planning and investment can lead to significant wealth, even in professions not typically associated with high earning potential. Teachers, with their profound impact on youth communities and their ability to inspire excellence both academically and athletically, have unique opportunities to supplement their income, particularly through summer engagements. This insight offered Chad a new perspective on how he could fulfill his passion while achieving financial success.

Mia is another example. After years in a corporate role, she realized that her true passion lay in environmental conservation. She took a bold step, leaving her stable job to volunteer with a local conservation group. Through this experience, she discovered a deep satisfaction in working outdoors and educating others about sustainability. This led her to pursue further education in environmental science, eventually securing a role with a local non-profit focused on regional climate change initiatives. Mia's journey wasn't without challenges, but her commitment to aligning her career with her values provided a sense of purpose and resilience. Her story illustrates the transformative power of pursuing a career that resonates with your calling, turning work into a rewarding and meaningful endeavor.

Similarly, there's Daniel, who pivoted from a high-pressure finance job to a career in graphic design. Driven by a lifelong love for art and creativity, he started consulting to build his skills. He then took on freelance projects alongside his day job, gradually building a portfolio. Daniel's dedication paid off when he landed a full-time role at a design agency, where he now thrives, blending his analytical skills with his artistic talents. This career shift required courage and perseverance, but the fulfillment he experiences now makes every effort worthwhile. Daniel's story is a testament to the idea that it's never too late to pursue a career that aligns with your true interests and values, leading to a more satisfying and balanced life.

In crafting a career that fits your calling, remember that the process is fluid and ongoing. Your interests and values may evolve, and your career path should adapt accordingly. Stay open to new opportunities and be willing to reassess your direction when needed. By keeping your core values at the heart of your career decisions, you create a professional life that sustains you financially and enriches you personally, weaving fulfillment and purpose into the very fabric of your work.

7.5 LEVERAGING TUITION REIMBURSEMENT BENEFITS

Tuition reimbursement programs are like hidden gems in the landscape of career development, offering a way to further your education without student loans. These programs are employer-sponsored perks that cover part or all of the costs associated with continuing education for traditional college courses, professional certifications, or necessary licensure. In a world where education often comes with a hefty price tag, tuition reimbursement provides a financial cushion, making it easier to pursue further studies. This support not only alleviates financial stress but also encourages employees to enhance their skills, ultimately benefiting both their personal growth and their employer's bottom line.

Understanding the eligibility and application process is crucial to making the most of these programs. Typically, employers have specific requirements that employees must meet to qualify for tuition reimbursement. These may include a certain tenure with the company or enrollment in courses that directly relate to your current job or future career within the organization. It's important to check with your human resources department to understand the specific criteria and deadlines. The application process usually involves submitting a formal request, detailing the courses you plan to take, and sometimes providing a rationale for how they will benefit your role. After completing your courses, you may need to provide proof of completion and grades to receive reimbursement. Being proactive and thorough in your application can streamline the process and ensure you receive the support you need.

The benefits of utilizing tuition reimbursement programs extend beyond immediate financial relief. They may allow you to focus on your professional development while working. Continuing education opens doors to career advancement. New qualifications and/or skills enhance your employability and positions you for promotions or new roles within your company. Employers often view employees who take initiative in their education as motivated and dedicated, making you more valuable in the competitive job market. Additionally, the knowledge and skills acquired through further education can lead to increased job satisfaction with greater competency and confidence in your abilities.

Several companies stand out for their commitment to supporting their employees' educational pursuits through robust tuition reimbursement programs. Starbucks, for instance, offers full tuition coverage for employees who enroll in Arizona State University's online degree programs. This initiative aids employees in obtaining a degree and aligns with the company's values of fostering growth and opportunity. Amazon's Career Choice program pre-pays 95% of tuition and fees for employees pursuing certificates and associate degrees in high-demand fields, demonstrating a forward-thinking approach to workforce development. These programs reflect a broader trend among companies recognizing the importance of investing in their employees' education, not just as a benefit but as a strategic investment in their workforce. Testimonials from employees who have taken advantage of these programs often highlight transformative experiences, both in terms of career progression and personal development, underscoring the profound impact of educational support.

7.6 BENEFITS OF RELOCATING FOR CAREER

Imagine receiving a job offer in a vibrant new state with endless opportunities. The prospect of relocating can be both thrilling and daunting, especially when you weigh the financial implications. On one hand, a move might lead to better career prospects, offering promotions or higher salaries that could significantly enhance your financial standing. On the other hand, it's crucial to consider the costs associated with such a transition. Moving expenses can add up quickly—think about hiring movers, transportation for your belongings, and potential storage needs. Then there are the transportation costs of getting yourself to the new location, whether by car, train, or plane. These expenses, though initially burdensome, can be viewed as an investment in your future, potentially leading to greater financial stability and career satisfaction.

Alongside direct moving costs, you must account for the differences in cost of living between your current location and your destination. Utilities, groceries, and taxes can vary, impacting your overall budget. Housing prices can vary widely for one area to another. A role that offers a substantial pay increase might seem attractive, but if it's in a city with a significantly higher cost of living, the financial benefits might not be as great as they initially appear. Conducting a thorough cost-of-living analysis before deciding to relocate can help you make an informed decision. Online cost-of-living calculators can provide a side-by-side comparison of expenses in different cities, helping you understand the financial landscape you're entering.

Beyond finances, relocation can have profound personal impacts, particularly on your social and family dynamics. Moving to a new state often means leaving behind a familiar support network of friends and family. The distance can strain relationships, requiring more effort to maintain connections. However, it also presents an opportunity to expand your social circle and immerse yourself in new cultures and communities. Adapting to a different environment involves embracing new customs, possibly learning a local dialect, and navigating unfamiliar settings. This cultural immersion can enrich your life, offering fresh perspectives and experiences that contribute to personal growth. While challenging, these adjustments are part of the broader adventure of relocation, offering a chance to redefine your identity and establish a sense of belonging in a new place.

Planning and executing a successful relocation involves careful research and strategic preparation. Start by thoroughly researching potential locations, considering factors like job market trends, community offerings, and lifestyle compatibility. Visiting the area before making a final decision can provide invaluable insights. Once committed, create a detailed relocation budget and checklist to manage all aspects of the move. This plan should include cost estimates for housing, transportation, and daily living expenses, as well as timelines for each phase of the move. Consider setting aside funds for unexpected expenses that might arise during the transition. Having a clear plan in place alleviates stress and ensures a smoother, more organized move.

Consider the story of Jake, who relocated from a small town to a bustling metropolis for a job opportunity. Initially apprehensive about the change, he meticulously planned his move, researching neighborhoods and calculating living expenses. Jake embraced the cultural diversity of his new city, joining local groups and attending community events to build a new social network. Professionally, the relocation paid off; Jake's career flourished in the dynamic environment. Looking back, Jake's experience broadened his horizons both personally and professionally. Similarly, Sarah moved to a different state to be closer to family while pursuing a career change. The transition required adjustments, but Sarah found fulfillment in her new role and appreciated the proximity to loved ones, enhancing her quality of life. These examples illustrate how thoughtful relocation can lead to personal and professional growth, even amidst the challenges of moving.

As you contemplate relocating, remember that the decision involves both financial and personal considerations. Balancing these factors requires introspection and planning, but the potential rewards can be significant. With the right mindset and preparation, relocation can be a stepping stone to new opportunities and experiences, enriching your life's tapestry and advancing your career in exciting ways. While complex, the process of relocation can serve as a catalyst for transformation, fostering resilience and adaptability in an ever-evolving world.

CHAPTER 8
ESSENTIAL FINANCIAL SKILLS FOR LIFE

Maintaining a good credit score requires understanding common pitfalls and how to avoid them. One of the most significant mistakes people make is maxing out their credit limits. High credit utilization can signal financial distress to creditors, harming your score. Another common error is neglecting to identify and correct your credit report of inaccuracies. Errors can appear due to clerical mistakes or even identity theft. Regularly checking your credit report helps you catch these issues early, allowing you to dispute them before they cause significant damage. Services like Experian, Equifax, and TransUnion offer free access to your credit reports annually, making it easy to stay informed.

8.1 CREDIT SCORE NOTES

To sustain a strong credit score, focus on consistent, responsible financial habits. Begin by making all payments on time. Late payments can severely impact your score, signaling unreliability to lenders. Set up reminders or automate payments to ensure you never miss a due date. Keeping your credit utilization low is another critical strategy. Even if you have a high credit limit, using only a small portion of it can positively influence your score. Avoid opening too many new accounts at once, as each application results in a hard inquiry on your report, potentially lowering your score.

Reflection Section: Credit Health Check

- Review: Take a few minutes to check your current credit score and report. Note any areas that need improvement.
- Plan: Set a specific goal for improving your credit score, whether it's reducing your credit utilization or ensuring timely payments.
- Action: Choose one actionable step, like setting up automatic bill payments, and implement it within the next week.

Establishing and maintaining good credit is an ongoing process, but the benefits are profound. A solid credit score improves your financial options and enhances your overall financial health. As you integrate these practices into your routine, you'll find that the world of credit is a conquerable behemoth and a manageable part of your financial life.

8.2 UNDERSTANDING TAX IMPACTS

Taxes may seem like a daunting topic, but understanding them is fundamental to managing your finances effectively. At their core, taxes are mandatory contributions levied by the government on individuals and corporations. These contributions fund public services and infrastructure essential for society. When you start earning, you'll encounter various types of taxes, each with its unique purpose and method of calculation. Income tax, perhaps the most familiar, is levied on earnings from jobs and investments. It's calculated based on your total income and determined by tax brackets, which decide the percentage you owe to the government. Then there's sales tax, added to the cost of goods and services at the point of purchase, varying by state and locality. Property tax is another type you might encounter if you own real estate, based on the value of your property and used to fund local services like schools and emergency services.

Filing tax returns is an annual ritual for most adults, documenting income, deductions, and credits to calculate the exact amount owed or refunded. It's crucial to file these returns accurately and on time to avoid penalties and interest. Understanding the importance of this process helps you plan your finances throughout the year. When you calculate your net income, which is your take-home pay after all taxes and deductions, you gain a clearer picture of your disposable income. This figure is pivotal for budgeting, saving, and spending decisions. Knowing how much you truly have at your disposal allows you to allocate funds more effectively, ensuring you meet financial obligations while setting aside money for future goals.

Taxes play a significant role in financial planning, influencing both income and budgeting. Planning for tax deductions and credits can minimize your tax liability, meaning you pay less in taxes. Deductions reduce your taxable income. For example, student loan interest and mortgage interest are common deductions that can lower your tax burden. Credits, on the other hand, directly reduce your tax bill on a dollar-for-dollar basis. Education credits for tuition, fees, and other educational expenses can be particularly beneficial for young adults. By understanding these options, you can effectively incorporate them into your financial strategy, ensuring you're maximizing potential savings.

Effective tax management requires strategic planning and organization. One approach is to utilize tax-advantaged accounts, such as Individual Retirement Accounts (IRAs) and Health Savings Accounts (HSAs). Contributions to these accounts can reduce your taxable income, offering a dual benefit of saving for future needs while decreasing current tax obligations. Keeping organized records throughout the year is essential for claiming deductions and credits. Maintain receipts and documentation for expenses related to education, medical bills, and charitable donations. This organization simplifies the filing process and ensures you don't miss out on potential savings.

Numerous resources are available to assist in managing your taxes efficiently. Tax preparation software like TurboTax and H&R Block can guide you through the filing process with user-friendly interfaces and step-by-step instructions. These platforms often offer features that automatically check for deductions and credits, minimizing errors and maximizing your returns. Interview tax professionals to understand their services and fees. Additionally, educational resources and workshops offered by local community centers or online platforms can further enhance your understanding of tax obligations and strategies. By leveraging these tools and resources, you can navigate the complexities of taxation with confidence and precision, ensuring your financial decisions are informed and advantageous.

8.3 EFFECTIVELY UTILIZING INSURANCE

Insurance may seem like an unnecessary expense until you find yourself in a situation where it becomes a lifeline. Think of it as a financial safety net, offering protection against unforeseen events that could otherwise cause severe financial strain. Whether it's an unexpected medical emergency or a car accident, insurance provides the necessary cushion to manage these situations without derailing your financial stability. Health insurance covers medical expenses, often the most unpredictable and costly. Auto insurance protects against losses from car accidents, ensuring you can get back on the road without financial ruin. Renters insurance safeguards your belongings from theft or damage within your rented home. Meanwhile, life insurance offers financial support to your loved ones in the event of your passing, covering debts and providing stability during challenging times.

Choosing the right insurance policy requires careful consideration of your personal circumstances and needs. Start by assessing what type of coverage you genuinely require. If you're a healthy young adult, you might prioritize a high-deductible health plan combined with a Health Savings Account, allowing you to save on premiums while still protecting against catastrophic events. For auto insurance, consider your vehicle's value and your driving habits. Automotive liability is generally required by law to protect others if you were to damage them. Collision and comprehensive coverage may protect or replace your assets. Renters insurance should reflect the value of your possessions, ensuring you can replace them if necessary. When comparing policies, pay attention to the terms and premiums. A lower premium might seem appealing, but higher deductibles or limited coverage could mean paying more out of pocket when you file a claim. Analyze the balance between cost and coverage to find a policy that meets your needs without breaking the bank.

Managing insurance costs is a critical component of maintaining financial health. One effective strategy is bundling policies. Many insurance providers offer discounts when you purchase multiple types of coverage through them, such as home and auto insurance. This bundling can result in significant savings while simplifying bill management. Another way to reduce premiums is by increasing deductibles. While this means you'll pay more upfront in the event of a claim, the monthly savings can be substantial, especially if you rarely file claims. It's crucial, however, to ensure you have enough savings to cover the deductible if needed. Regularly reviewing your policies and shopping around for competitive rates can also yield savings. Loyalty to one provider doesn't always translate to the best rates, so it pays to compare options periodically.

Real-life examples illustrate the profound impact insurance can have. Consider Sarah, who faced a major medical emergency. Her health insurance covered the bulk of the expenses, sparing her from insurmountable debt. Without it, she would have faced a financial crisis, unable to afford necessary treatments. Then there's Alex, whose apartment was burglarized. Thanks to his renter's insurance, he was able to replace his stolen laptop and other valuables, preventing the disruption from escalating into a financial setback. As a young adult, Dustin became a testicular cancer survivor. His health insurance covered the bulk of cancer treatment and allowed him to continue and thrive financially. These stories highlight that while insurance requires upfront costs, the benefits in times of need far outweigh the premiums paid.

For some, the concept of self-insurance becomes appealing as financial independence grows. This approach involves taking on the financial responsibility typically covered by insurance, relying instead on personal savings and investments. The goal is to build enough wealth so that you no longer need life insurance after retirement, as your accumulated assets can support your dependents. Self-insurance requires intentional financial planning over many years, focusing on building a robust financial portfolio. While it's not suitable for everyone, it offers hope for those seeking to minimize monthly expenses in retirement. By understanding and effectively utilizing insurance, you pave the way for a secure financial future, protecting your assets and your peace of mind.

8.4 LIFE INSURANCE AND WILLS

Imagine you're the main breadwinner with loved ones relying on your income to maintain their lifestyle. Suddenly, the question of what would happen if you were no longer there becomes vital. This is where life insurance steps in, providing a financial safety net for those who depend on you. Whether it's a spouse, children, or business partners, life insurance ensures that your financial contributions continue even in your absence. Determining if others depend on your income can help you decide the necessity and extent of coverage. If you have dependents, securing a policy that covers at least ten times your annual income is advisable. This amount can function as an endowment, allowing your beneficiaries to live off the investment growth. For those with a mortgage, a 20 or 30-year term may align with the time frame needed to pay off the home, providing peace of mind that housing stability is ensured.

Securing life insurance isn't just about the present; it evolves as your life and career do. When you land a better job or your income significantly increases, it's crucial to revisit your life insurance policy. Consider layering an additional policy to ensure your coverage remains at ten times your total income. This adjustment not only reflects your current financial status but also protects your growing responsibilities and future aspirations. While the idea of purchasing more insurance might seem daunting, it's a proactive step in safeguarding your family's future. Additionally, term life insurance tends to be more affordable, allowing you to adjust coverage without straining your budget. It's a small price for the security of knowing your loved ones remain financially protected.

While contemplating life insurance, it's equally important to think about what happens to your assets. Creating a simple will is an often-overlooked step in financial planning, yet it's crucial for ensuring your wishes are honored. A will outlines how your assets are distributed, who will care for your children, and who will execute your estate. If you have assets, a spouse, or dependents, a will is not just a good idea —it's essential. Without one, the distribution of your estate is left to state laws, which is always cumbersome and may not align with your intentions. Thankfully, creating a will isn't complicated or expensive. Online platforms offer state-specific templates that guide you through the process, allowing you to create a legally binding document in the comfort of your home. These services provide a straightforward way to ensure that your legacy is handled according to your wishes. Document a will when you have assets or dependents; replace it by creating another whenever or when you move to a new state.

Taking the time to establish life insurance and a will is a demonstration of care, ensuring that those you leave behind are equipped to handle the financial challenges that may arise. It's an act of responsibility that offers peace of mind, knowing your loved ones are supported. While these topics might not be the most comfortable to discuss, addressing them head-on is an empowering step in securing your financial future. As you continue to explore the various facets of financial planning, remember that the decisions you make today lay the groundwork for a secure tomorrow.

8.5 AVOID INVESTING GIMMICKS

In the realm of investing, the allure of quick gains often tempts many into risky ventures. Single stocks, gold, and so-called "get rich quick" schemes sometimes promise high returns, but they rarely deliver long-term success. These investments can be volatile, with single stocks swinging dramatically on market whims and gold fluctuating based on global events. While they might seem like a thrilling ride, they often end up being more like a rollercoaster, with steep climbs followed by stomach-churning drops. The uncertainty of such investments can wreak havoc on your financial stability, leaving you vulnerable in times of need. It's akin to gambling—sometimes you win, but more often than not, you lose. This unpredictability is why seasoned investors often advise against putting all your eggs in one basket, especially baskets as precarious as these.

One of the more deceptive traps in the financial world is cash value life insurance, which combines elements of insurance and investment. Products like whole life, universal life, or variable life insurance may sound appealing with promises of savings growth alongside coverage. However, these are often poor choices for investment. The complexity of these policies can mask their inefficiencies, with high fees and low returns compared to traditional investment avenues. Instead of seeing tangible growth, policyholders may find their money tied up in a product that doesn't yield the expected benefits. It's much like buying a car with a fancy paint job but a faulty engine—it looks good on the outside, but under the hood, it's not worth the price. For those looking to grow their wealth, separating insurance from investment is usually the wiser course. By investing in straightforward, low-cost funds and maintaining simple term life insurance, you can effectively manage your financial goals without the hidden costs and complexities.

The timeless wisdom of Aesop's fable "The Tortoise and the Hare" rings true in the world of investing. The tortoise, with its steady and deliberate pace, ultimately wins the race. This parable underscores the importance of patience and consistency in financial growth. The tortoise's approach mirrors successful investment strategies—focusing on wise, long-term endeavors rather than chasing fleeting trends. When you invest your time and money in solid, sustainable opportunities, you build a foundation that withstands market turbulence. It's about the diligent accumulation of wealth over time, not the frantic pursuit of immediate riches. This mindset helps protect your investments from the latest fads that often promise more than they can deliver. Staying informed and skeptical of too-good-to-be-true opportunities shields you from financial pitfalls and keeps your portfolio on a steady path.

In today's fast-paced financial landscape, new trends and investment opportunities pop up frequently, each claiming to revolutionize wealth-building. However, the core principles of investing remain unchanged: diversification, steady growth, and risk management.

These fundamentals are your best allies in navigating the investment world. By avoiding gimmicks and focusing on proven strategies, you ensure your financial journey is not just a series of impulsive decisions but a well-thought-out plan. This approach might not offer the excitement of a high-stakes gamble, but it provides something far more valuable—stability and peace of mind. In investing, as in life, the slow and steady truly does win the race.

8.6 SEEKING PROFESSIONAL FINANCIAL ADVICE

Navigating the financial landscape can feel like exploring a dense forest without a map. This is where professionals come in—they're your guides, equipped with the expertise to help you chart a course through the complexities of personal finance. An investment advisor, for example, can be invaluable, providing you access to major investing platforms and offering insights into building a diverse portfolio tailored to your financial goals. They can help you evaluate risk, understand market trends, and select investments that align with your long-term vision. Meanwhile, a non-captive insurance agent can be your ally in finding the right insurance policies. Unlike captive agents, who represent a single company, these agents shop across multiple providers to secure the best coverage and rates for your unique needs. This flexibility ensures that you're not just getting a one-size-fits-all policy, but something that's truly personalized.

When it comes to taxes, licensed CPAs (Certified Public Accountants) are the experts you want in your corner. They do more than prepare your taxes—they offer strategies for tax efficiency, helping you keep more of your hard-earned money. Whether it's navigating the nuances of deductions or understanding the implications of new tax laws, a CPA's guidance can be pivotal. Similarly, real estate brokers provide expertise when you're ready to buy or sell property. Their knowledge of market conditions, property values, and negotiation strategies can make a significant difference in these high-stakes transactions. By leveraging the expertise of these professionals, you gain access to informed, unbiased advice that can simplify complex financial situations and enhance your decision-making process.

Choosing the right advisor is crucial, and there are a few key criteria to consider. Start by checking credentials and certifications. For investment advisors, look for a Certified Financial Planner (CFP) designation, which indicates rigorous training and adherence to ethical standards. For tax-related needs, a CPA credential is essential. Understanding the fee structure is also important. Some advisors work on a commission basis, which means they earn a percentage from the products they sell, while others charge a flat fee or an hourly rate. A fee-only advisor might offer more impartial advice, as they aren't incentivized to promote specific products. By carefully evaluating these factors, you can select a professional who not only meets your needs but also aligns with your values and financial philosophy.

For those who prefer a DIY approach or want to supplement professional advice, there are alternatives available. Online financial planning tools and robo-advisors offer automated, algorithm-driven financial planning services with lower fees. These platforms can help you manage investments, create budgets, and plan for retirement with minimal human interaction. Financial literacy workshops and community programs provide education on a wide range of topics, from budgeting basics to advanced investment strategies. These resources empower you to make informed decisions and build your financial knowledge over time. By incorporating these tools into your financial strategy, you can gain a deeper understanding of your finances and make informed decisions with confidence.

Real-life testimonials highlight the transformative power of professional advice. Take the story of Lisa, who struggled with debt for years. After consulting a financial advisor, she implemented a debt reduction strategy that gradually improved her financial situation. Within a few years, she was debt-free and had started saving for retirement. Or consider Tom, who worked with a CPA to optimize his tax strategy. The result was significant savings each year, which he reinvested into his business, fueling its growth. These stories underscore the value of seeking expert guidance, illustrating how professional advice can lead to successful financial outcomes and empower you to achieve your goals.

CONCLUSION

As we reach the end of our journey together, I want to take a moment to reflect on the path we've traveled. Throughout this book, we've explored the fundamental pillars of financial independence—from mastering the art of budgeting to navigating the complex world of investing. We've delved into the importance of financial literacy, the power of responsible money management, and the strategies to break free from the shackles of debt. These themes, interwoven throughout our discussions, form the bedrock of a sound financial future.

I began this book with a simple vision: that financial independence is within reach for every young adult. It's not a privilege reserved for the wealthy or the lucky few. It's a goal that each of you can achieve through dedication, discipline, and the right tools. The strategies and insights we've covered are not mere theories; they are practical, actionable steps that you can implement starting today. Whether it's creating a zero-based budget, building an emergency fund, or investing in your first retirement account, every small action contributes to the larger picture of your financial well-being.

As you embark on this journey, remember the key takeaways that will guide you along the way. Embrace the power of budgeting to take control of your money. Commit to a debt-free lifestyle. Recognize that investing is not a realm reserved for experts, but a tool accessible to anyone willing to learn. These insights, coupled with the practical steps outlined in each chapter, form a roadmap to financial success.

But knowledge alone is not enough. It's time to take action. Start by setting up a budget that aligns with your goals and values. Pay off all debts except a home mortgage. Establish your emergency fund. Then invest 15% of your annual income towards retirement. Remember, every journey begins with a single step, and the sooner you start, the greater the rewards will be. Never take out another car loan or extended warranty. Protect from catastrophe with auto, home and health insurance. When you have assets or dependents, invest in a will and term-life insurance.

As you progress on this path, know that you are not alone. The pursuit of financial independence is a shared journey, and there is a vibrant community of like-minded individuals ready to support and inspire you. Engage with this community, share your experiences, and learn from the wisdom of others. Remember, financial education is a lifelong process. Continue to seek out resources, attend workshops, and stay curious about the ever-evolving landscape of personal finance.

I want to thank you for joining me on this journey. Your commitment to improving your financial well-being is a testament to your strength and determination. As you close this book, know that you hold the power to shape your financial future. Embrace the challenges, celebrate the victories, and never lose sight of the ultimate goal—a life of financial freedom and abundance.

I invite you to stay connected, to share your stories, and to be a beacon of inspiration for others embarking on this path. Together, we can create a generation of financially empowered young adults, ready to tackle the challenges of the future with confidence and resilience.

Remember, your financial journey is unique, and there will be obstacles along the way. But armed with the knowledge, strategies, and mindset we've explored, you have the tools to overcome any hurdle. Believe in yourself, stay committed, and never stop learning. The future is yours to create, and I have no doubt that you will achieve the financial independence you deserve.

So, my friends, go forth with courage, with determination, and with the knowledge that you hold the key to your financial destiny. The journey ahead is filled with possibilities, and I can't wait to see the incredible heights you will reach. Thank you for being a part of this transformative adventure. Here's to your financial freedom and a future filled with abundance!

KEEPING THE GAME ALIVE

Now that you have the tools to take control of your finances, ***it's time to pass on what you've learned*** *and help someone else start their journey.*

Simply by sharing your honest thoughts about this book, you can guide other young adults toward financial confidence—just like you found here. ***Your review could be the reason someone finally starts budgeting, opens their first investment account, or avoids a costly mistake.***

Thank you for your support. ***Financial knowledge grows when we share it****, and you're helping me make sure that every young person has the chance to build a secure and independent future.*

Scan the QR code to leave a review:

Your voice matters. Let's keep the momentum going!

*– **Clay Kennington***

REFERENCES

- 20SomethingFinance. (n.d.). *Contentment versus upgrade consumerism.* 20SomethingFinance. https://20somethingfinance.com/contentment-vs-consumerism/
- Aquent Talent. (n.d.). *Finding fulfillment at work: Aligning your career and core values.* Aquent Talent. https://aquenttalent.com/blog/finding-fulfillment-at-work-aligning-your-career-and-core-values
- Bankrate. (n.d.). *The psychological benefits of paying off debt.* Bankrate. https://www.bankrate.com/personal-finance/debt/psychological-perks-of-debt-payoff/
- Community College Research Center. (n.d.). *New federal transfer data: Which colleges are serving transfers?* CCRC. https://ccrc.tc.columbia.edu/easy-blog/federal-transfer-data-which-colleges-serving-transfers.html
- Consumer Financial Protection Bureau. (n.d.). *An essential guide to building an emergency fund.* CFPB. https://www.consumerfinance.gov/an-essential-guide-to-building-an-emergency-fund/
- Discover. (n.d.). *4 tips for budgeting on an irregular income.* Discover. https://www.discover.com/online-banking/banking-topics/4-tricks-for-budgeting-on-a-fluctuating-income/
- Experian. (n.d.). *Should I finance or pay cash for a car?* Experian. https://www.experian.com/blogs/ask-experian/should-i-finance-or-pay-cash-for-a-car/
- Experian. (n.d.). *Why is it important to establish credit when young?* Experian. https://www.experian.com/blogs/ask-experian/why-it-is-important-to-establish-credit-when-you-are-young/
- Forbes. (2024, April 2). *How to decide if a job relocation is worth it.* Forbes. https://www.forbes.com/sites/tracybrower/2024/04/02/how-to-decide-if-a-job-relocation-is-worth-it/
- Forbes Finance Council. (2024, May 21). *The role of emotional intelligence in financial decision making.* Forbes. https://www.forbes.com/councils/forbes-financecouncil/2024/05/21/the-crucial-role-of-emotional-intelligence-in-financial-decision-making/
- Going Merry. (n.d.). *How to get scholarships: 12 essential tips for standing out.* Going Merry. https://goingmerry.com/blog/how-to-get-scholarships/
- Hedge & Sachs. (n.d.). *Investing for beginners: How to manage your investment risk.* Hedge & Sachs. https://hedgeandsachs.com/investing-for-beginners-how-to-manage-your-investment-risk/
- Internal Revenue Service. (n.d.). *401(k) plan overview.* IRS. https://www.irs.gov/retirement-plans/plan-sponsor/401k-plan-overview
- Investopedia. (n.d.). *10 tips for managing your student loan debt.* Investopedia.

https://www.investopedia.com/articles/personal-finance/082115/10-tips-managing-your-student-loan-debt.asp

- Investopedia. (n.d.). *Zero-based budgeting: Benefits and drawbacks.* Investopedia. https://www.investopedia.com/ask/answers/051515/what-are-advantages-and-disadvantages-zerobased-budgeting-accounting.asp
- Kids Financial Education. (n.d.). *Best financial apps for teens and young adults.* Kids Financial Education. https://www.kidsfinancialeducation.com/best-financial-apps-for-teens-and-young-adults/
- National Association of Realtors. (n.d.). *Housing statistics and real estate market trends.* NAR. https://www.nar.realtor/research-and-statistics/housing-statistics
- NBC News. (n.d.). *This couple used the debt snowball method to pay off $130,000 in four years.* NBC News. https://www.nbcnews.com/better/life-style/couple-used-debt-snowball-method-pay-130-000-four-years-ncna1059086
- NerdWallet. (2025). *The best budget apps for 2025.* NerdWallet. https://www.nerdwallet.com/article/finance/best-budget-apps
- NerdWallet. (n.d.). *How much house can I afford?* NerdWallet. https://www.nerdwallet.com/calculator/how-much-house-can-i-afford
- Rocket Mortgage. (n.d.). *15 first-time home buyer tips.* Rocket Mortgage. https://www.rocketmortgage.com/learn/first-time-home-buyer-tips
- Rocket Mortgage. (n.d.). *Buying a fixer-upper house: Pros and cons.* Rocket Mortgage. https://www.rocketmortgage.com/learn/pros-cons-buying-fixer-upper-house
- Salience Health. (n.d.). *Manage student loan stress.* Salience Health. https://saliencehealth.com/news/manage-student-loan-stress/
- Sunshine Coast Credit Union. (n.d.). *How to achieve your goals with a simple financial roadmap.* Sunshine Coast Credit Union. https://www.sunshinec-cu.com/create-a-simple-financial-roadmap-to-stay-on-track
- U.S. News & World Report. (n.d.). *College majors with the best return on investment.* U.S. News. https://www.usnews.com/education/best-colleges/articles/college-majors-with-the-best-return-on-investment
- United Way NCA. (n.d.). *Youth financial literacy: Why is it important?* United Way NCA. https://unitedwaynca.org/blog/financial-literacy-for-youth/
- Vanguard. (n.d.). *Roth IRA vs. traditional IRA: Eligibility, rules, and tax benefits.* Vanguard. https://investor.vanguard.com/investor-resources-education/iras/roth-vs-traditional-ira

APPENDIX

Monthly Budget Worksheet
Young Adult Financial Planning

Budget For: ____________ Month Of: ____________

Prepared Date: ____________ Revised Date: ____________

Monthly Income

	Name:	Amount:
Income Source 1		
Income Source 2		
Income Source 3		
Income Source 4		

Monthly Total Income: $

Monthly Spending:

	Name	Amount		Name	Amount		Name	Amount
Giving:			Living:			Saving:		

Subtotal $ Subtotal $ Subtotal $

Monthly Total Spending: $

*Income - Spending Zero Based Budget: 0 *Must be zero

Irregular Income Budget
Young Adult Financial Planning

Budget For: ____________________

Prepared Date: ____________________

Prioritized Budget Categories

1	Groceries	$	________
2	Utilities	$	________
3	Mortgage Payment	$	________
4	Transportation	$	________
5	Charitable Giving	$	________
6	Healthcare	$	________
7	Entertainment	$	________
8	Miscellaneous	$	________
9	Restaurant	$	________
10	Tuition	$	________
11	Savings	$	________
12	Peaks and Valleys Fund		________

Monthly Total Expenses: **$**

Steps:
Prioritize Budget Items by importance
As irregular income arrives, pay down the list item by item

Snowball Debt Payoff

Young Adult Financial Planning

Debt Snowball for: ______________________

Prepared Date: ______________________

Debt Account	Payoff Amount	Monthly Payment	Month 1	Month 2	Month 3	Month 4	Month 5	Month 6
	$	$	$					
	$	$	$					
	$	$	$					
	$	$	$					
	$	$	$					
	$	$	$					
Monthly Payoff:								

Net Worth Calculator — Young Adult Financial Planning

Net Worth of: ______________________

Prepared Date: ______________________

	Account	Amount		Debt Type	Amount
Assets		$	Liabilities		$
		$			$
		$			$
		$			$
		$			$
		$			$
		$			$
		$			$
		$			$
		$			$
	Asset Subtotal	$		Liabilities Subtotal	$

*Assets-Liabilities **Current Net Worth:** $

www.ingramcontent.com/pod-product-compliance
Lightning Source LLC
LaVergne TN
LVHW022005200926
848481LV00007B/2237